GENIUS GYMNASIUM

by Ivan Moscovich

Sterling Publishing Co., Inc.
New York

2 4 6 8 10 9 7 5 3 1

Published by Sterling Publishing Co., Inc.
387 Park Avenue South, New York, NY 10016
© 2006 by Ivan Moscovich
Distributed in Canada by Sterling Publishing
c/o Canadian Manda Group, 165 Dufferin Street,
Toronto, Ontario, Canada M6K 3H6
Distributed in the United Kingdom by GMC Distribution Services,
Castle Place, 166 High Street, Lewes, East Sussex, England BN7 1XU
Distributed in Australia by Capricorn Link (Australia) Pty. Ltd.
P.O. Box 704, Windsor, NSW 2756, Australia

Printed in China

Sterling ISBN-13: 978-1-4027-3373-4
       ISBN-10: 1-4027-3373-9

For information about custom editions, special sales, premium and
corporate purchases, please contact Sterling Special Sales
Department at 800-805-5489 or specialsales@sterlingpub.com.

Book design by Judith Stagnitto Abbate / Abbate Design

CONTENTS

Introduction 4

How To Use This Book 6

Creative Thinking Puzzles 9

Logic Puzzles 31

Number Puzzles 53

Visual Reasoning Puzzles 73

Word Puzzles 99

Answers 123

Genius Gymnasium Training Program 171

INTRODUCTION

The Genius Gymnasium offers a program of mental exercises to tone, train, boost, and bolster the five main fields of active mind power.

In the first *Genius Gymnasium* program, we concentrate on the active mental skills you can develop to build your brainpower in ways that will make you fighting fit for any mental challenge. The only technique we're not including here is memory training, for the same reason that physical fitness programs don't normally include power lifting techniques. Memory training is great for building pure mental muscle, but memory doesn't necessarily help you think, and that's what the *Genius Gymnasium* is all about.

Our program emphasizes creative thinking which, like circuit training in a regular gym, is a great way to build flexibility, lasting mental stamina, and all-round mental fitness. Creative thinking liberates that fundamental human drive—curiosity—and with curiosity unleashed, the gifts of mental youth and mental usefulness soon appear.

The first group of mental circuit training exercises sets graded challenges to coach you in *creative thinking* and so provide a foundation on which the other sections can build. The puzzles will refine the natural puzzle-solving aptitudes released by everyone's latent creativity. But, once released, creativity needs other mental skills to achieve its full potential.

Logic is the first of these. It was recognized by the Ancients and reached its highest stature in the schools of Ancient Greece. The skill of logic is still taught in schools of philosophy today, recognized for the precise and potent mental discipline it provides. The second training sequence in this book focuses on logic puzzles, and clearly demonstrates how this rigorous mental training can also be fun.

The art of *Numbers* is the second of these mental skills. It, too, reached a pinnacle of excellence in Ancient Greece but has continued to evolve to this day, and many masters of the art—because it is an art as much as it is a science—believe its fullest flowering has barely begun. The art of numbers can also be called the art of mathematics, in which numbers play a central and crucial role. Numbers themselves are symbols, shorthand signs like letters, or the quick lines that sketch a painter's thought. Playing with numbers is also fun, as the graded number puzzles in this book will show.

The third skill that enhances creativity is *Visual Reasoning.* Psychologists suggest that our visual perception works in a different way than our logical and numerical mind. Certainly, experience shows that some people have a greater facility for solving visual problems than number problems while others have the reverse, although whether this difference comes from natural aptitude or education is still an open question. Visual thinking and problem solving, which combine in visual reasoning, involve much more than just solving puzzles of colors and shapes; therefore the puzzles in the third set of exercises are carefully chosen to challenge and stretch this frequently underused aspect of our brains.

Word Puzzles encourage the last of these four enormously important skills that support, enhance, and develop our creative mental powers. This skill is the power of words, of language itself. Words allow us to express our thoughts. Even more, they are the building blocks with which ideas are formed. Creativity is molded by the words we have, or inhibited by the absence of the words we cannot find. Words are also the key to humor—and whenever we have fun playing with words we are refining our creative skills at the same time.

Creativity is a child of curiosity and, like humor, it is commonly a quick and natural response to something unexpected. We smile when we make the connection, whether we have just spotted the solution to a problem we've been wrestling with, or whether we have just gotten a joke.

HOW TO USE THIS BOOK

This book is written to represent a gymnasium and training ground for the genius that can be found in all of us, and this is why we have called it the *Genius Gymnasium*. It contains 125 specially selected and created puzzles grouped into five categories and graded in five levels.

The first group focuses on creative thinking, which we regard as the most important mental skill of all, because if you think creatively, mental challenges of all kinds can be tackled more effectively.

Each of the four other groups of puzzles focuses on mental skills that support, enhance, and strengthen creative thinking in different ways.

The mental exercise program in the *Genius Gymnasium* is based on a combined approach that develops and builds your mental muscles in a holistic, self-supporting way. To guide you, we provide a scheme so you cannot only assess your mental strengths and weaknesses, but also measure your pace of improvement as you follow the program.

Stage 1: Start with the simplest puzzles at Level 1. Tackle one puzzle a day from each category for five days, so that by the end of the first week you have completed all the puzzles graded as Level 1.

Stage 2: Rest for two days to let your brain catch up and consolidate the skills you have learned.

Stage 3: In the second week, tackle the puzzles graded as Level 2, five puzzles a day, one from each category, so that you have solved all the Level 2 puzzles by the end of the second week.

Stage 4: Then take two days off from puzzle solving, so the unconscious part of your brain can do its work while you rest.

Stages 5, 6, 7, 8, and 9: Repeat this process for each level of difficulty, up from the next level (Level 3) to Level 4 and finally to Level 5, tackling five different kinds of puzzle each day for five days, then resting for two days before moving on to the next level the following week.

In this way you will complete the course, working steadily through each level, starting with the easiest at Level 1 and ending at Level 5.

Even after the first week you'll be sure to notice the difference in your puzzle solving facility . . . so imagine how good you'll be when the end of the fifth week has come!

Because there are so many different kinds and levels of puzzle, it's hard to measure your improvements against these puzzles themselves. Also, the benefits in this mental exercise program are not only focused on solving puzzles, but on improving your brainpower in all kinds of different ways. Use the charts at the end of the book to record the time you take to solve each puzzle, and you'll find that you get to be as quick or even quicker solving the puzzles at Level 5, when you get there, as you were solving the puzzles at Level 1—and that's a real achievement! You can be proud of how much your brainpower has improved by your five-week workout at the *Genius Gymnasium*.

CREATIVE THINKING PUZZLES

Brainpower benefits you can get from these puzzles include:
Mental flexibility; creativity; intuition; lateral thinking power.

SHAPE UP

Creative thinking comes from a combination of intuition and clarity. This puzzle is a good way to see how the two can both help and hinder each other.

Which of the following are true and which are false? If you think it depends, state what conditions are necessary for the statement to be true.

1. All squares are rectangles.

2. A triangle can have two obtuse angles.

3. The diagonals of a rectangle cross at right angles.

4. When you double the side of a square you double the area.

5. A parallelogram has rotational symmetry of order 4 (can be rotated on a 90° angle without changing the object).

6. The longest side of a triangle is shorter than the sum of the lengths of the other two sides.

7. If two rectangles both have the same area, they must also have the same perimeter.

8. A rhombus is a parallelogram.

9. Four infinitely long straight lines cross at six different points.

Answers on page 124

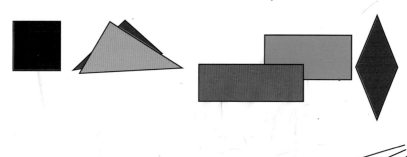

LOST IN SPACE

This huge space station is constructed from 39 giant spherical modules, interconnected by a network of transparent cylindrical passages as shown below.

In their spare time, the intergalactic crew and visitors try to traverse the whole space station, visiting each module and never retracing their journey through the interconnecting passages. Is this possible, and, if so, how can it be done?

Your task is to re-create their journey, starting at one of the modules and, without lifting your pencil from the page, visiting each module at least once but without going over any interconnecting channel more than once.

Some of the interconnecting passages may be left untraversed.

Answer on page 124.

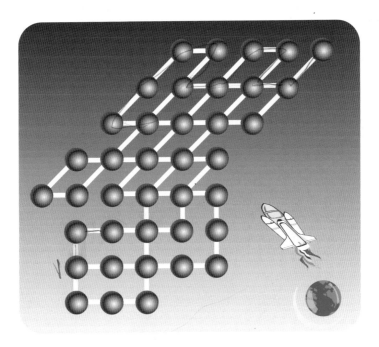

ALL ROADS LEAD FROM HOME

You live at the top left corner of the map and work in an office at the point shown in Gridlock City. How long is the shortest path to your office, and how many different routes to work are there that require driving the minimal distance?

Hint: Start with a smaller journey, then look for a rule.

Answer on page 125

Office

L
E
V
E
L

1

WINDOW OF OPPORTUNITY

It took the maid too much time to clean the window, so her employer ordered a new one, giving the builder exact instructions: The new window should give half the light, it should be a square, and it should be the same height and width as the present window. How did the builder solve the problem?

Answer on page 126

L
E
V
E
L

1

ELUSIVE ELLIPSE?

How can this man, sitting near his desk, create an ellipse without touching his pen, ruler, compass, or computer?

Answer on page 126

INEBRIATED INSECT

Two ladybugs landed on my glass: one outside, exactly in the middle of the glass, the other exactly opposite but inside the glass. The height of the glass is 5 ½ inches and the width is 4 inches. Can you describe the shortest path from one to the other? Are you able to estimate how long that path is?

Answer on page 126

PERFECT GOLOMB RULER

An unusual measuring idea is the concept of the Golomb ruler. A Golomb ruler is a ruler constructed in such a way that no two pairs of marks on it can measure the same distance. The markers on a Golomb ruler must be placed at integer multiples of a fixed spacing. The markers must be placed so as to achieve as many distinct measures of distances between two markers as possible, with a given number of markers.

In a perfect Golomb ruler of length n, all the distances 1–2–3–...n can be measured exactly once, while in an optimum Golomb ruler (or the shortest Golomb ruler possible for a given number of marks), the condition remains that no two pairs of marks can measure the same distance, but the ruler may not have all consecutive distances from zero to the ruler's length.

The puzzle behind a perfect Golomb ruler is finding out how to place marks on a line so that all the whole number units from 1 to the total that make up the length of the ruler can be measured.

The 2-unit length ruler above with 3 markers is not perfect, since it can measure a 1-unit distance in two ways. A 3-unit length ruler with 3 markers is the first perfect ruler.

Can you do better and create a perfect Golomb ruler with 4 markers? (For convenience, we will say that each end of the ruler requires a marker.) What will its length be and where should the 4 markers be placed? The first marker has been placed for you, but where should the next 3 be placed?

Hint: Not all the squares are used, so the length is less than 10.

Answer on page 127

0   10

SPHERE
OF INFLUENCE

Imagine you have a thin-walled glass sphere filled with water fitting exactly into a cubical box, the width and height of which exactly match the diameter of the sphere.

If you break the glass sphere and pour the water into the cube, how much of the cube's volume will be filled with water?

Answer on page 127

L
E
V
E
L

2

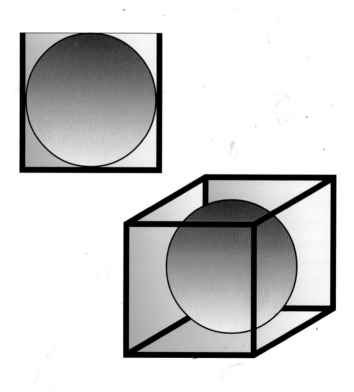

GOT YOU PEGGED

The upper pegboard has some pegs that fit into the holes in the lower board. Just by looking, can you work out the maximum number of pegs that will fit into the holes at once? How many pegs will be left free?

Answer on page 128

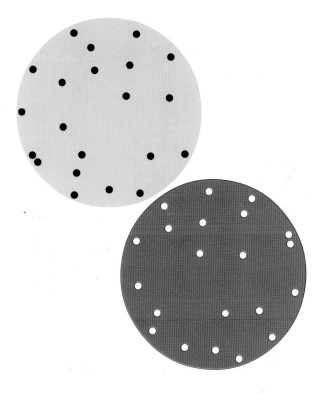

FLAG THE FLY

The lizard starts at the bottom of the grid and moves along the intersections in an attempt to catch the fly shown at the top. His moves can be of any of the three types shown in the inset.

How might he do it? (A path is demonstrated above that falls short of the fly by only three square units.)

Answer on page 128

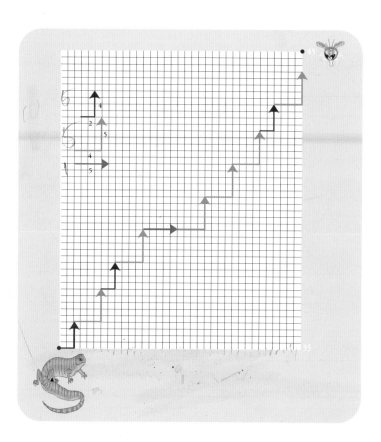

TRANSFORMABLE CYLINDER

The upper disk of this transformable cylinder is fixed to the ceiling, while the lower disk is freely suspended on stretched rubber bands. What will the structure look like when the lower disk is rotated 90 degrees clockwise or 180 degrees counterclockwise? Can families of straight lines create curved surfaces?

Answer on page 129

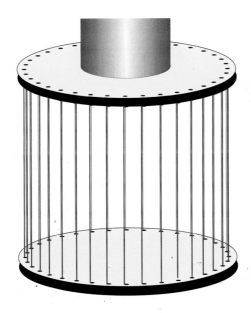

SCHLEGEL'S SHORTCUT

Starting at the corner shown, can you find a route for the snail along the edges of this three-dimensional solid object that will visit each corner only once, with no edge retraced? Such a route is called a Hamiltonian circuit.

It can be cumbersome to solve such problems looking at the three-dimensional representation of objects, because some edges and corners are hidden. So to help you we have created a topologically equivalent two-dimensional representation of the object, called a Schlegel diagram, on which the solution can be more easily worked out.

Answer on page 129

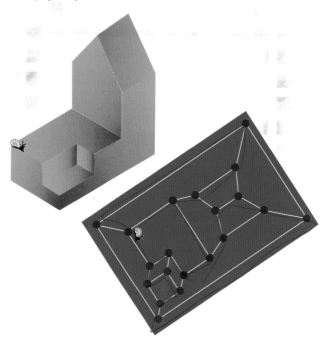

TREASURE HUNT

Treasure is hidden at one of the intersections of the city of Gridlock. You have randomly chosen an intersection and have received secret information: The treasure is hidden on a diamond with eight street intersections on each side, the center of which is six blocks east from your chosen point, and on one of the intersections that make up the given green diamond. How many trial digs will be needed, at most, to pinpoint the intersection where the treasure is hidden?

Answer on page 130

Answer on page 130

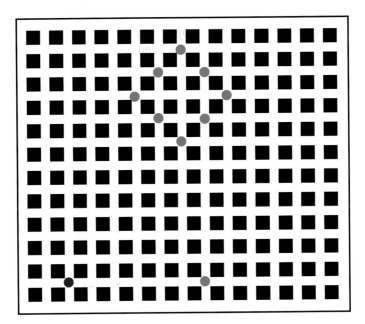

○ your randomly chosen point

○ the center of the circle on which the treasure is hidden

○ given circle

DEER, OH DEER!

The magician Mel Stover challenged me with this puzzle one day over breakfast at one of Martin Gardner's gatherings in Atlanta.

Change only one single matchstick to let the Bambi look in another direction without changing its shape in any way.

Reflections and rotations are allowed. It took me quite a while to find the solution.

Answer on page 130

DOGGED DETERMINATION

This playful dog was not careful enough and was hit by an automobile. Fortunately, he wasn't too badly hurt and was taken to a vet.

By changing the positions of only two matchsticks, can you visualize how he looked on the vet's table?

Answer on page 130

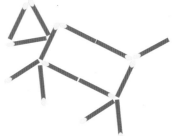

THE SHORT AND LONG OF IT

The schematic diagram below shows the road network between a set of towns.

Mathematically, it is called a tree graph. The colors of the roads indicate their length rounded off to the nearest 5-mile increment.

1. Can you find the longest possible distance between any two towns (without taking any U-turns)?

2. Generally, this kind of problem can challenge even the most advanced computers, especially if the number of towns increases. Can you describe a simple way to demonstrate which path through the network is longest without resorting to any math?

Answer on page 131

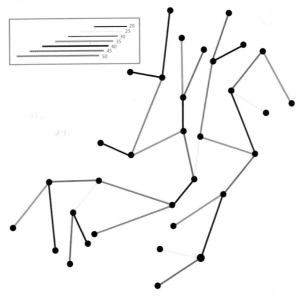

PERFECT GOLOMB RULER TOO?

Five markers are placed on a ruler of 11-unit length. It is a Golomb ruler since no two pairs of markers measure the same distance. But is the ruler perfect? Can you measure all consecutive distances from 1 to 11 between any two markers, each distance, in only one way? Or, is it the shortest optimum Golomb ruler for five markers? (See the explanation of perfect versus optimum Golomb rulers on page 15.)

Answer on page 132

0   1   11

GANYMEDE CIRCLE 1

If a Golomb ruler is bent so the ends are joined together, this is called a Ganymede circle. The aim in this puzzle is to place three marker discs on points around the circle so that all distances from 1 to 7 units can be measured as distances between one marker and another. (For consistency, measure clockwise each time.)

Where should the three markers be placed?

Answer on page 132

GANYMEDE CIRCLE 2

The circumference of the circle is divided into 13 parts. Place four marker points along the circumference so that every distance from 1 to 13 will correspond to a distance between two marker points.

Answer on page 133

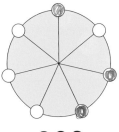

1. ●●●

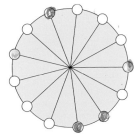

2. ●●●●

GANYMEDE CIRCLE 3

The circumference of the circle is divided into 21 parts. Place five marker points along the circumference so that every distance from 1 to 21 will correspond to a distance between two marker points.

Answer on page 133

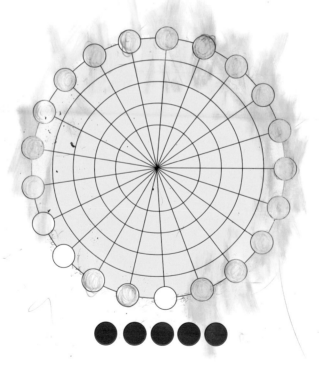

I SPY

The vigilant interplanetary security officer below followed an intruder on his computer screen. The alien spyship entered his planetary system at one of the three planets located at the uppermost part of the screen, and in one continuous path crossed all the established routes between the planets (indicated by yellow circles). He travelled every route, collecting secret information on the way, never taking a route more than once, and with the obvious intention of leaving the system as soon as he completed his mission. But defense forces are waiting at the point of his intended departure, and the chances of escape are slim.

Can you guess at which planet the interplanetary defense forces are waiting?

Answer on page 134

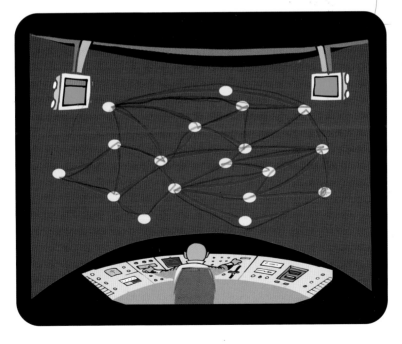

MONTY HALL PROBLEM

You have been selected to participate in a game show that offers you the chance to win a luxury automobile. The automobile is behind one of the three doors. A goat is behind each of the other two. You must choose a closed door. The host (who knows where the automobile is) does what he always does: He opens an unpicked door to show a goat (there's always at least one unpicked door with a goat behind it to open). He then offers you the choice of switching doors if you wish. To switch or not to switch—that is the question.

Answer on page 135

THE MONK AND THE MOUNTAIN

A monk climbs a mountain along a narrow track. He starts at seven in the morning and reaches the top at seven in the evening. His route follows a narrow serpentine path, at varying rates of speed and with many stops. The next morning he starts going down at the same time and along the same route and reaches the bottom again at the same time in the evening.

Is there a spot along his path that the climber will have occupied on both trips at precisely the same time of the day?

Answer on page 136

BANK RAID

In the two-dimensional space of Flatland, there is a bank whose vault is an ingenious mechanism consisting of four sliding linkages which can move up, down, left, and right only.

The four black squares are fixed at the four corners of the rectangular vault and the sliding linkages cannot cross them. The object is to remove the four linkages, one on each side of the vault, to uncover the vault completely.

Which piece must be moved first? How many moves will it take you to open the vault?

Answer on page 137

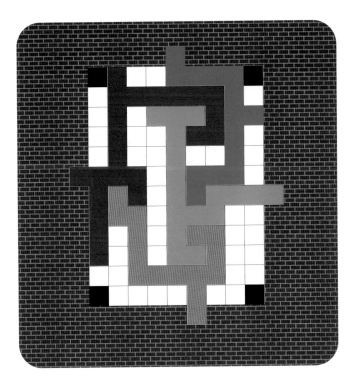

PICTURE STRIP

A picture is hidden in the pattern. Can you discover the secret
principle on which the picture was hidden, and figure out what it depicts?
Answer on page 138

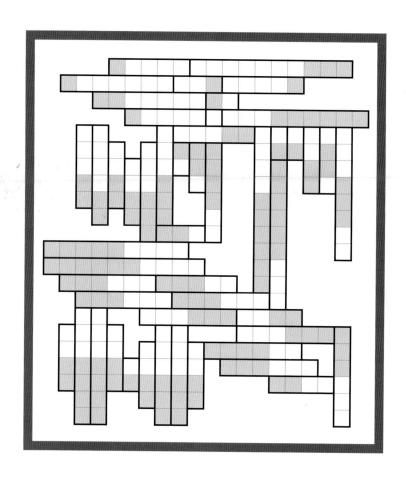

LEVEL
5

LOGIC PUZZLES

Brainpower benefits you can get from these puzzles include:
Precision skills; clarity awareness; critical judgment; analysis power.

STAINED GLASS WINDOW

Some panes are missing from this stained glass window. What color should they be?

Answer on page 138

RIGHT TO THE EDGE

How many colors will you need to color each straight line between two gray endpoints so that no two lines of the same color meet at any endpoint?

Answer on page 138

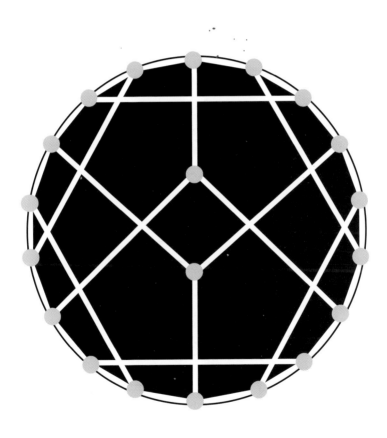

L
E
V
E
L

1

FIRE DRILL

At a recent fire a fireman stood on the middle rung of a ladder directing water into the burning building. As the smoke diminished, he stepped up three rungs and continued his work from that point.

A sudden flare-up forced him to descend five rungs. Later he climbed up seven rungs and worked there until the fire was out.

Then he climbed the six remaining rungs and entered the building.

How many rungs were there on the ladder?

Answer on page 139

STARRY SKY

Looking at a starry sky, how many stars do you have to select to guarantee that you can make a convex pentagon when you connect them with straight lines?

Seven stars selected, as shown, won't solve the puzzle, no matter how the lines are connected. Endre Makai proved the theorem to solve this problem.

Answer on page 139

Convex polygons

A polygon is convex if you can draw a straight line between any two points that remain inside the shape.

Convex   **Not Convex**

ALIEN-NATION

The population of the world in 2999 is dominated by aliens and consists of either aliens or human beings dressed in alien disguise.

The aliens are incapable of telling a lie, and the human beings are all equally incapable of telling the truth.

The being on the left (1), identifies himself to the one in the middle (2), who tells the one on the right (3): "He says he is an alien."

"No, he is not an alien—he is a human being," answers the one on the right (3).

Can you tell whether there are more aliens or human beings in the group?

Answer on page 139

1   2   3

FAR TRAVELED

Can you choose any of the cities below, then make an all-inclusive round-trip? The aim is to visit all the cities, then return to the city from which you started, always following the directions indicated by the arrows on each line and never retracing the lines. For example, what will be the order of the round-trip starting and ending with New York and visiting all the cities?

Answer on page 140

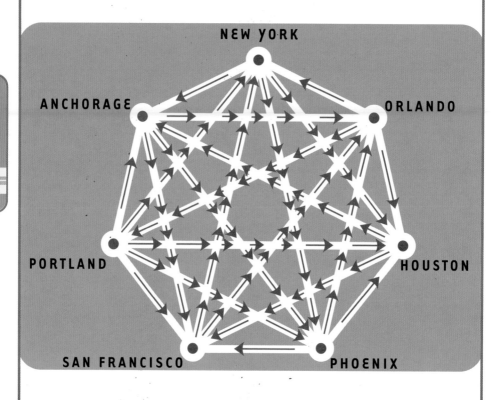

ZOO-LOGICAL

The 7-by-5 unit rectangular area of the zoo has been divided into eight fenced regions to house the animals as shown.

Can you work out the sizes of the eight areas?

Answer on page 140

CHOP CHOP

At a birthday party, three cakes are cut as shown below and divided between two groups, one group getting the red parts, and the other the yellow parts. Did both groups get an identical share of each cake?

Cake 1 is cut through the center, making six identical 60-degree angles, with the six pieces divided between two groups of three children. Cake 2 is cut through a point off-center, again making six identical 60-degree cuts and divided as before. Cake 3 is cut through the same off-center point as cake 2, but making eight identical 45-degree angles, and divided this time between two groups of four children.

Answer on page 140

The cuts

cake 1   cake 2   cake 3

BE FLIPPANT

What is the probability of getting two tails and two heads in succession when flipping a coin?

Answer on page 141

MOLE

The mole starts from the red point, with the red line showing its path until its end at the blue point.

Can you work out the logic of its path until the point at which it changed the rule? At which point did this happen?

Answer on page 141

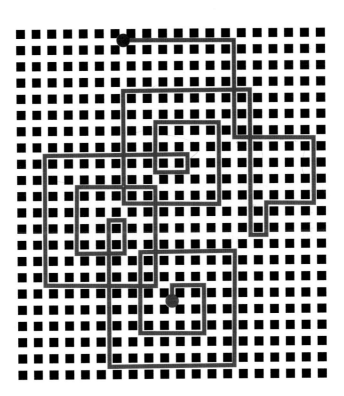

Can you visit the 14 circles within the map in succession along a continuous line, visiting each circle just once and returning to the point from which you started?

Answer on page 142

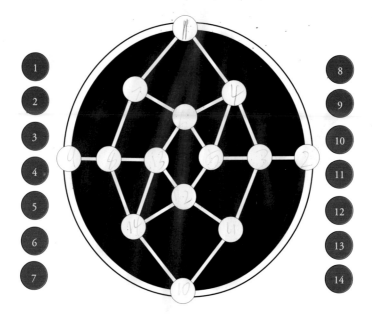

EULERIAN PATHS

Euler's theorem is as follows:

1. A graph has an Eulerian circuit if and only if it is connected and all of its vertices are even;
2. A graph has an Eulerian path if and only if it is connected and has either no odd vertices or exactly two odd vertices. If two vertices are odd, then any Eulerian path must begin at one of the odd vertices and end at the other.

Take a look at the road network below. Starting at any point (A to J) that you choose, is it possible to drive over each road exactly once, thus creating an Eulerian path? Furthermore, is it possible to end up where you started from, thus forming an Eulerian circuit?

Answer on page 142

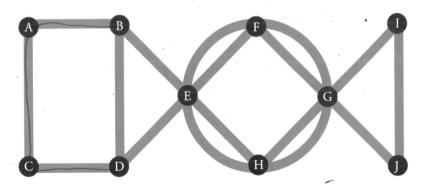

ONE FOR THE BIRDS

In a cage are red birds and blue birds. Each red bird sees as many red birds as there are blue birds. Each blue bird sees three times as many red birds as blue birds. How many red and blue birds are in the cage?

Answer on page 143

RECONNAISSANCE

The high-altitude reconnaissance plane crossed the red boundary 12 times before returning to its home base. The next time it wanted to make a similar mission, but it wanted to cross the boundary only 11 times before returning.

Can you suggest a path for such a mission?

Answer on page 143

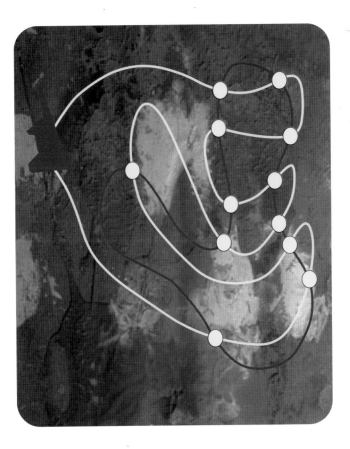

HAPPY END PROBLEM

Once again looking at a starry sky, how many stars do you have to select to guarantee that you can make a convex quadrilateral when you connect four of them with straight lines?

Four stars selected as shown won't do.

Hungarian mathematicians Esther Klein and Gyorgy Szekeres were the first to prove the theorem for this convex quadrilateral problem. It was named the Happy End Problem by another Hungarian mathematician, Paul Erdös, after the two were married.

Answer on page 143

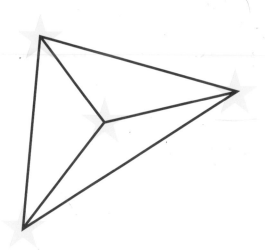

PIPELINE PUZZLE

Can you color all the lines between two points using four colors, so that four differently colored lines meet at every point? To play as a game, players take turns coloring lines. The first player unable to legally color a line loses the game.

Answer on page 144.

LOCAL LIQUOR

A bar frequently visited by 12 friends living in the city of
Gridlock (their homes are indicated on the map by black circles) is situated
at a spot minimizing the total walking distance for all of them taken
together. At which of the two marked spots is the bar situated? A or B?

Answer on page 144

T-HAT'S MAGIC!

The magician put four yellow, four green, and four red eggs in each of two hats. He called a person up from the audience, blindfolded him, then asked him to transfer five eggs from hat 1 to hat 2.

The magician then asked the audience to tell the blindfolded assistant how many eggs have to be returned to hat 1 to ensure that in hat 1 there will be at least three eggs of each of the three colors. What is the answer?

Answer on page 144

CATERING FOR THE CHILDREN

At this birthday party three cakes have to be cut by vertical straight-line cuts into exactly 34 pieces and divided among 34 excited children.

Puzzle 1

What is the minimum number of straight-line cuts needed to ensure that each child gets a (not necessarily identical) piece of cake? There is one condition: Each cake has to be cut by at least two cuts. Under this condition can each child get a piece of a cake?

Puzzle 2

What would be the minimum number of pieces and cuts needed if we change the problem so that it is now necessary to cut the three cakes into identical pieces (but again, with straight-line cuts) so that each child gets a piece of cake?

Answer on page 145

cake 1   cake 2   cake 3

ID PARADE

In a police lineup arranged according to height, Mac stood exactly in the middle.

His jailmate Nick was higher up, in the 13th position, and another, Jim, was even higher, at the 20th position.

Given that each inmate was different in height, how many inmates took part in the lineup?

Answer on page 146

DELIVER THE GOODS

In Gridlock City the pizza boy must make five deliveries from the pizza shop located at point 1 to five other locations (2, 3, 4, 5, and 6 as shown). The blocks in Gridlock City are all of the same size. What will be his best route starting from the pizza shop and returning again, visiting each location just once, but in any order?

Here's a suggested approach for you to try: Work out the minimum distances between each set of locations, then find out which route will allow you to visit them all in the smallest distance.

Answer on page 146

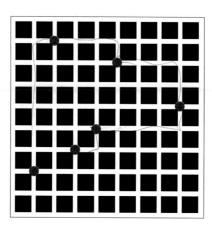

A SHAKER'S DOZEN

Twelve friends meet and shake hands with each other. How many handshakes are there altogether in this exchange of greetings?

Answer on page 147

GOLDEN HANDSHAKE

At the board meeting there were 17 board members, each of whom was supposed to shake hands with every other person. But four members did not shake hands with each other. How many handshakes took place?

Answer on page 147

LET'S SHAKE ON IT

My wife and I invited four married couples to our housewarming party. Just before everyone left, I asked everyone else how many people they had shaken hands with. I received the following replies: 8, 7, 6, 5, 4, 3, 2, 1, and 0. Given that no one shook hands with his or her own spouse and no pair of people shook hands more than once, can you tell how many times my wife must have shaken hands with a guest?

Answer on page 147

L
E
V
E
L

5

FLASHPOINT

The bridge pictured will collapse in exactly 17 minutes. The four hikers must cross the bridge in that time in pitch darkness. They have only one flashlight among them, which is needed for each crossing.

A maximum of two people can cross the bridge at one time carrying the flashlight, which must be returned by hand after each crossing.

Each hiker walks at a different speed: One takes 1 minute to cross, another takes 2 minutes, and the others take 5 and 10 minutes respectively. Each pair crosses the bridge at the rate of the slower hiker's pace (so, for example, hiker 1 crossing with hiker 3 will cross the bridge in 5 minutes).

No tricks are allowed: The flashlight cannot be thrown back, no hiker is allowed to carry another, etc.

There are two possible solutions. Can you find either of them?

Answer on page 148

NUMBER PUZZLES

Brainpower benefits you can get from these puzzles include:
Numerical skills; sequence and relationship recognition;
combination awareness; calculation power.

GET THE MESSAGE?

Messages like these were sent to outer space in order to establish communication with intelligent life, beings who would be unlikely to understand our written or spoken languages.

For this reason, interstellar messages use only mathematical language and binary codes. Can you decipher the message below?

Answer on page 148

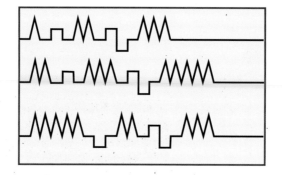

L
E
V
E
L

1

MAGIC ARROWS

Sixteen arrow tiles with arrows in different orientations can form a great number of different configurations. A number overlay has been placed around a game board. The object of this puzzle is to find a corresponding configuration of the 16 arrow tiles.

The 16 arrow tiles have to be placed on the game board (the black points indicate the top of the tile) in such a way that the number of arrows pointing to each number on the card will match that number on that card. Can you complete the game we've started below on the game board?

Answer on page 148

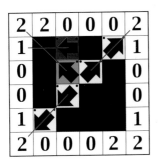

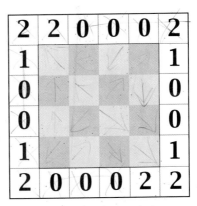

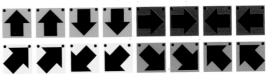

LEVEL 1

SWEEEET

A piece of cake and a sundae cost two and a half dollars together, but the cake costs a dollar more than the sundae.

How much does each cost?

Answer on page 149

A SUITE DEAL?

The saleslady sold two sofas at the bargain price of $1,200 apiece.

She made a 25% profit on the first sofa and took a 20% loss on the other. She assumed that she still made a profit on the combined sale. Was she right in this assumption?

Answer on page 149

TIM'S TURTLE

Tim found 14 bricks from which to construct a wall in the garden for his new pet, a small turtle.

As his turtle grew, Tim wanted to enlarge the enclosure as much as possible, using the same number of bricks. How could he do this?

Answer on page 149

ST. IVES' RIDDLE

Ahmes's puzzle on page 71 has inspired many variations, among them the St. Ives riddle. Leonardo of Pisa (otherwise known as Fibonacci) published the rhyme in 1202 in his Liber Abaci. The rhyme is as follows:

"As I was going to St. Ives, I met a man with seven wives. Every wife had seven sacks. Every sack had seven cats. Every cat had seven kits. Kits, cats, sacks, and wives. How many were going to St. Ives?"

Answer on page 149

WHO IS A MILLIONAIRE?

Three of these people are celebrating their millionth birthdays. One has lived for a million hours, the other a million minutes, and the third a million seconds. Can you identify their approximate ages? Which person is the odd one out?

Answer on page 149

TOT UP A TON

Can you arrange the digits from 1 to 9 in order, using each digit once only and inserting plus and minus signs as needed, to produce the sum of 100?

Answer on page 150

SCHOOL BUS 1

Three children are waiting for the
school bus. Two of them, a brother and his
little sister, always hold hands and board
the bus one after the other. In how many
different ways can the three children board
the bus?

Answer on page 150

SCHOOL BUS 2

The next day a fourth child joins the
waiting children. In how many·
different ways can the four children
board the bus? How many ways are
there when a fifth child joins the
queue?

Answer on page 150

THE FIRST CONTACT

Mathematics is the only universal language that we could expect intelligent aliens to understand.

The best way to establish communication with aliens is by mathematics, as in the message in the puzzle, "Get the Message?" is on page 54 (reprinted below). If we received the message below in response, would it indicate that our message had been understood?

Answer on page 150

MESSAGE SENT

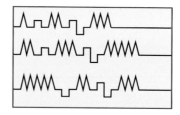

MESSAGE RECEIVED

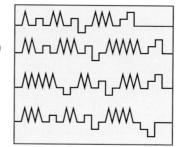

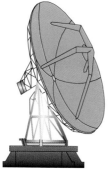

SNAIL'S PACE

74

A little snail climbed up a window 90 units high. If every day it climbed up 11 units, and every night it dropped back 7 units, and it climbed every day without fail, how many days did the little snail take to reach the top?

Answer on page 151

L
E
V
E
L

3

GOLDEN JUBILEE

The king has ordered a golden plaque of his profile for a commemorative celebration.

He was presented with three plaques, each one of identical thickness and proportions but of different sizes.

The width at the neck was 13, 12, and 5 units respectively.

Which required more gold to make: the two smaller heads or the big head only?

Answer on page 151

SKYDIVING 1

Four skydivers are practicing for a big show. Three of them, the ones with red parachutes, are a bit superstitious and always jump one after the other. In how many different ways can the four skydivers jump from the airplane?

Answer on page 151

SKYDIVING 2

More skydivers are joining the team of four: In how many different ways can five of them jump? How about six? Remember that the three members of the red team always jump one after the other.

Answer on page 152

PUZZLE WITH A TWIST

This emergency escape staircase for the helipad structure is in the form of a helix spiral, travelling exactly four times around the building as shown.

The circumference of the round building measures 40 units and the height is 120 units.

Can you figure out the length of the spiral staircase?

Answer on page 152

AN UP AND DOWN CAREER

In this 20-floor building there is only one strange elevator, which has just two buttons: one up and the other down. The up button takes you up eight floors (or doesn't move at all if there are not eight floors available), and the down button takes you down 11 floors (or doesn't move if there are not 11 floors available).

Is it possible to get from the ground to any floor by taking the elevator?

How many times will the maintenance man have to push the buttons to get from the ground to all the other floors and in what sequence will he visit the floors?

Answer on page 152

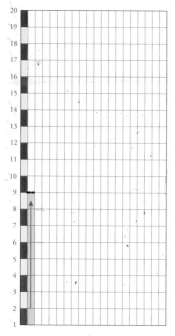

PIPE BAND

Nine pipes are tied tightly together by a red metal band. How long is the band?

Answer on page 153

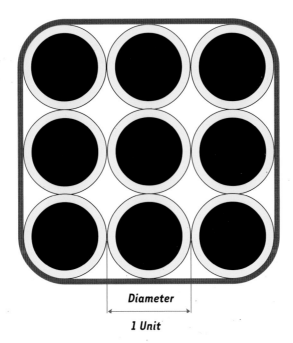

Diameter

1 Unit

THE SHOELACE PROBLEM

What is the best way to lace your shoes? A few different ways are shown for a shoe with six pairs of eyelets.

Which of the four ways below is the shortest and which is the longest way to lace the shoe, if the laces must alternate between eyelets on the left and right side of the shoe?

Answer on page 153

 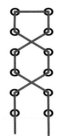  

| Zigzag (American) | Bow tie lacing | Straight lacing (European) | Quick lacing (Shoe shop) |

COMMUTER COMPUTATION

Yesterday, I traveled to work at my usual average of about 56 mph. However, coming home there was construction holding up the traffic, so on my return journey I averaged only 28 mph.

What was my average speed for the round trip?

Answer on page 153

GRASSHOPPING

Given a line of integral length n, the object is to start jumping from point 0, in successive jumps of consecutive lengths: 1-2-3 . . . n along the line, so as to make as many jumps as possible and finish the nth jump at the end of the line, at point n. Jumps are allowed in both directions along the line.

The first five games are demonstrated (from $n = 1$ to $n = 5$). We can see that apart from the trivial $n = 1$ line, a complete jump ending at n was achieved only on line $n = 4$. Can you find out the next two lengths on which complete jumps ending at the end of the line can be achieved?

Answer on page 153

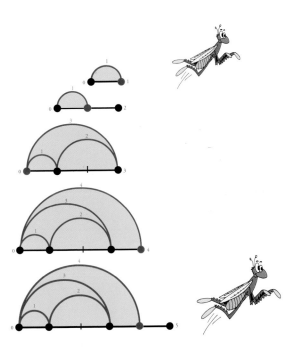

THE SAFE SAFE

A safe has four dials, each with the 26 letters of the alphabet, and is opened by a four-letter code in which each letter can be used only once. The order matters, so XBFG is different from GXBF. Do you think it would be easy for a thief to figure out the secret code? If it takes five seconds to try each possible combination, how long do you think it would take to try them all?

Answer on page 154

SKELETON CUBES

Twelve different-colored rods of equal length can be magnetically attached to form a cube as shown.

Can you figure out how many differently colored cubes you could form from the 12 magnetic rods?

Answer on page 154

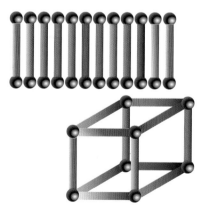

L
E
V
E
L

5

HISTORY MYSTERY

Seven houses each have seven cats. Each cat kills seven mice. Each of the mice would have eaten seven ears of wheat. Each ear of wheat would have produced seven bags of flour. How many bags of flour were saved by the cats? (This puzzle dates from 1850 B.C, from the ancient Egyptian Rhind papyrus, written by Ahmes.)

Answer on page 154

LEVEL
5

PLANT PLOT

Problems involving arrangements of a number of points (*n*) in various intersecting lines—so that exactly a certain specified number of them (*k*) will be on each line—are often known as "tree planting" problems. The objective is to maximize the number of lines (*r*).

Can you find a solution where 13 points ($n = 13$) are to be arranged over 9 lines ($r = 9$) with four points on each line ($k = 4$)?

Answer on page 154

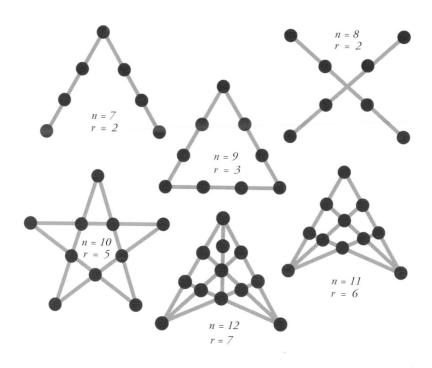

n = 7
r = 2

n = 8
r = 2

n = 9
r = 3

n = 10
r = 5

n = 11
r = 6

n = 12
r = 7

VISUAL REASONING

Brainpower benefits you can get from these puzzles include:
Shape and color perception; spatial awareness;
pattern recognition; right-brainpower.

PLAYGROUND

You are looking from above at a playground on which planks are piled one on top of another. Can you identify the highest point?

Answer on page 155

THE CIRCLE INSIDE

These four equal squares have sides of length 2r.
Which figure has the largest black region?
Answer on page 155

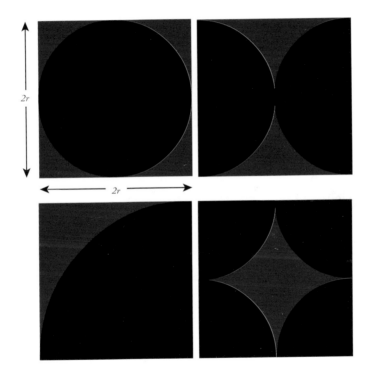

L
E
V
E
L

1

MYSTERY SHAPE

Can you find the missing shape here?
Answer on page 155

LEVEL

1

HERE'S THE PLAN 1

Select the set of orthographic projections corresponding to the iso-metric drawing of object A.

Answer on page 155

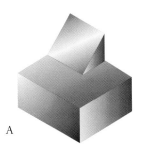

A

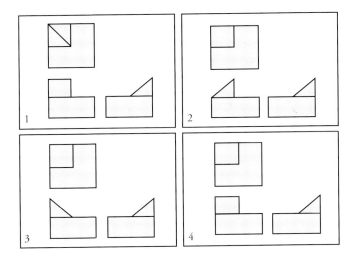

L
E
V
E
L

1

Select the set of orthographic projections corresponding to the iso-metric drawing of object B.

Answer on page 155

B

LINEUP

How many lines will you be able to trace from the left side of the diagram to the right, just by looking, before you lose track? Stability of attention is required. This is the ability to direct your attention for a long period toward something, combined with resistance to fatigue and distraction.

Answer on page 156

L
E
V
E
L

2

FELINE A BIT PECKISH

These nine small, colored birds are in danger of being eaten by the big hungry cat below. How many birds can be eaten by the cat (in other words, how many birds can be placed in the outline of the cat, without overlap)?

Answer on page 156

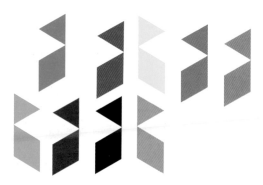

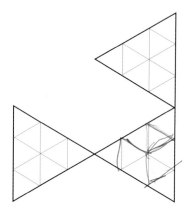

LEVEL 2

TO THE MAX

Which of these six triangles on the sides of a regular hexagon has the greatest area?

Answer on page 156

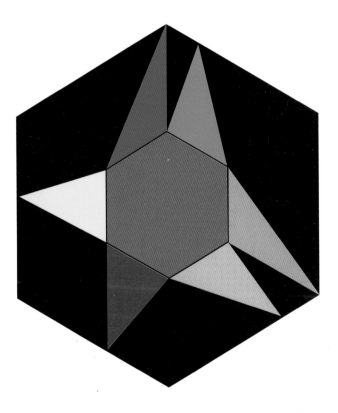

Select the set of orthographic projections corresponding to the iso-metric drawing of object C.

Answer on page 156

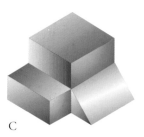

C

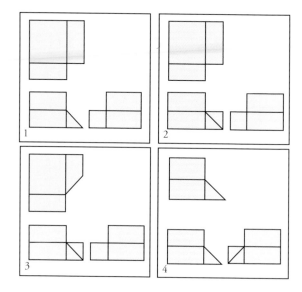

HERE'S THE PLAN 4

Select the set of orthographic projections corresponding to the iso-
metric drawing of object D.

Answer on page 156

D

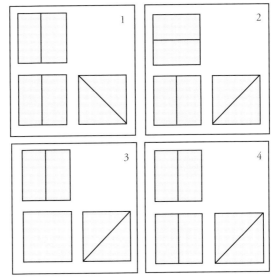

CHEESE, PLEASE

If you had a spherical piece of cheese and took a very thin, flat slice through it at any angle, you would always obtain a circular disc of cheese.

Take a look at the three pieces of cubical cheese we have for you below. They have been hung at different angles. If you were to take thin, horizontal slices through these cubical cheeses, which of the shapes shown could you obtain? Which are impossible?

Answer on page 157

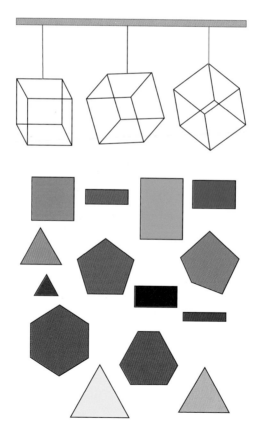

HIDDEN POLYGONS

How many regular polygons and stars can you count in the circle?

Answer on page 157

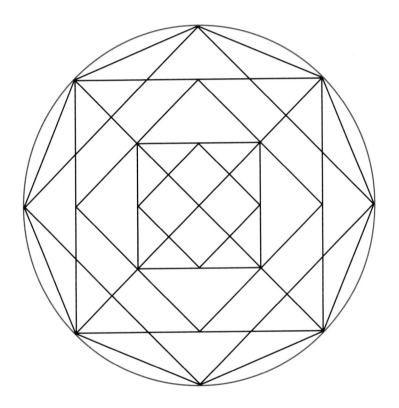

PAPER VIEW 1

A square piece of paper is folded in half, and half again, as shown below.

Differently shaped holes are cut through the folded piece as shown in the examples below.

When the pieces are unfolded, select the correct pattern obtained from the four given colored alternatives.

Answers on page 158

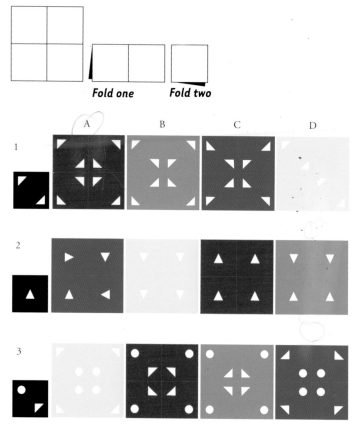

Fold one   **Fold two**

HERE'S THE PLAN 5

Select the set of orthographic projections corresponding to the iso-metric drawing of object E.

Answer on page 158

Answer on page 158

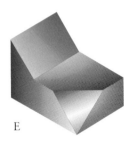

E

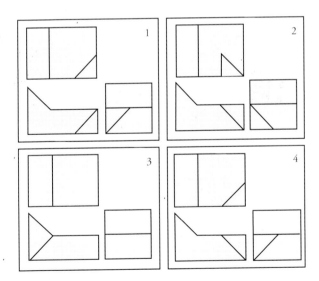

Select the set of orthographic projections corresponding to the iso-metric drawing of object F.

Answer on page 158

F

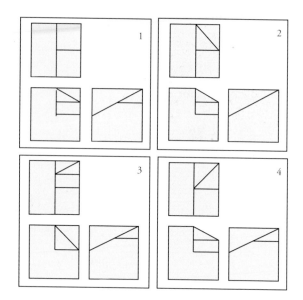

THE HINGED SQUARE

The hinged square transformation of Henry Ernest Dudeney is a real gem of recreational geometry. He dissected a square into four parts. Hinges, represented here as black circles, connect the parts to each other. If you leave the blue piece fixed and swing the others around their hinges, you can rearrange the pieces to form a new shape. Just by looking, can you guess what the new shape will be?

Answer on page 158

PAPER VIEW 2

This time a rectangular piece of paper is folded as shown below.

Again, differently shaped holes are cut through the folded piece as shown in the examples.

The pieces are then unfolded. Can you select the correct pattern obtained from the three given colored alternatives?

Answers on page 158

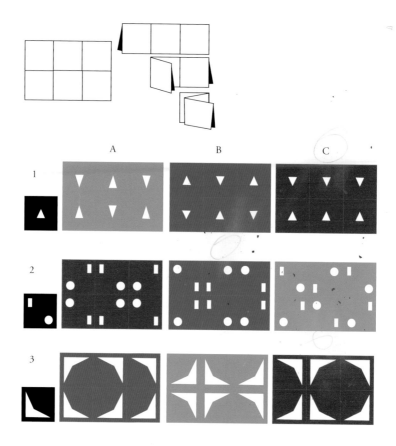

TWENTY-FIVE SENSE

How many consecutive straight line connections (moving horizontally and vertically) can you make between two adjacent points without crossing your path, starting from the point shown? Points may be reused.

Answer on page 158

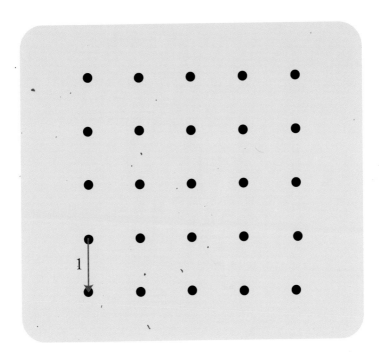

HERE'S THE PLAN 7

Select the set of orthographic projections corresponding to the iso-metric drawing of object G.

Answer on page 159

G

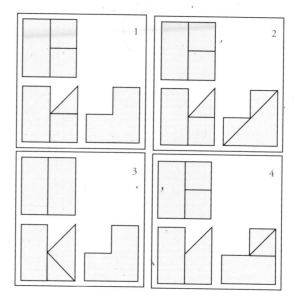

HERE'S THE PLAN 8

Select the set of orthographic projections corresponding to the isometric drawing of object H.

Answer on page 159

H

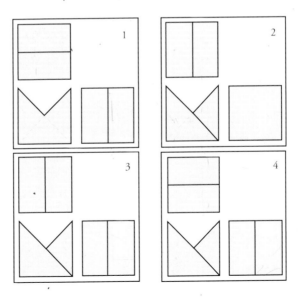

LADYBUG IN HIDING

The bird at top left is looking for a nice, juicy ladybug that she saw crawling around on these leaves. The ladybug started on the leaf shown at bottom then traveled once across every available overlap between one leaf and an adjacent leaf. She stopped when there were no new "overlaps" to visit. As a result, she visited every leaf in the maze once, except for the junctions, which she visited twice. Under which leaf is the ladybug hiding?

Answer on page 159

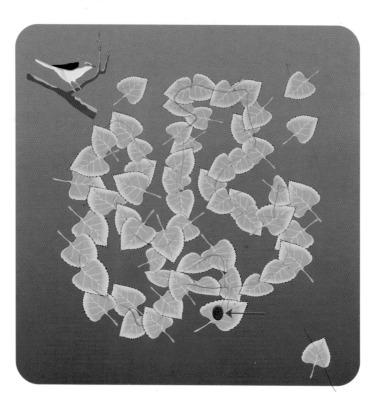

SWEET SIXTEEN

Six straight lines are needed to create a continuous line through a square of 16 points, as shown below.

Puzzle 1
Can you find any of the other 13 possible solutions?

Puzzle 2
How many solutions can you find that have the smallest number of intersections of the lines?

Puzzle 3
How many solutions can you find that form symmetrical patterns?

Answers on page 160

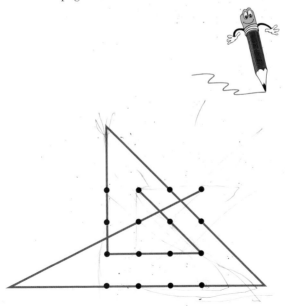

L
E
V
E
L

5

BLANKET COVERAGE

This intricate tessellation consisting of triangles, squares, pentagons, hexagons, heptagons, and octagons was created from one single element. Can you determine what it is and how the pattern was created?

Answer on page 160

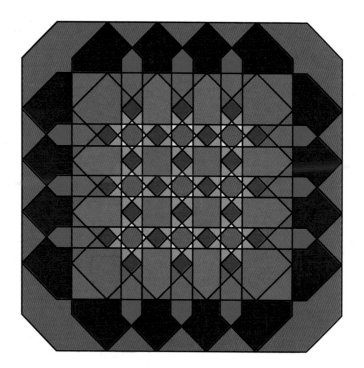

LEVEL

5

STOPGAPS

Just by looking, determine which of the colored shapes fit each of the gaps in the black and white columns. Place your answers in the table below.

How many mistakes did you make? You may be surprised!

Answer on page 160

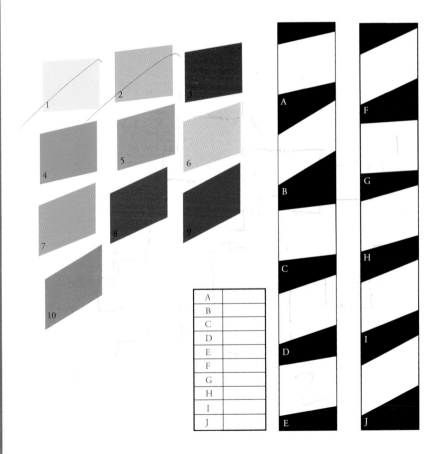

A	
B	
C	
D	
E	
F	
G	
H	
I	
J	

FOUR-WAY MAZE

Start at one of the four arrows. Move from square to square horizontally or vertically according to this sequence: Yellow, red, green, blue.

Repeat this sequence until you reach the center, avoiding black squares. The center square may be reached from any color square. Which arrow leads to the shortest route to the center?

Answer on page 161

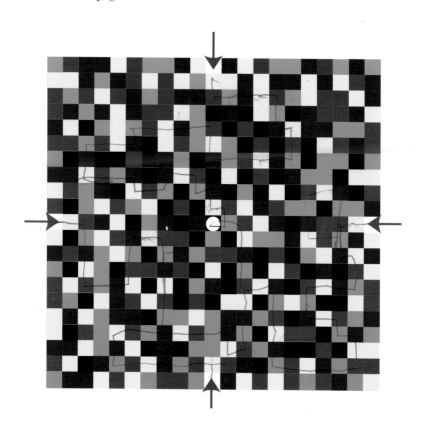

WORD PUZZLES

Brainpower benefits you can get from these puzzles include:
Language recognition; spelling and vocabulary skills;
communication awareness; left-brainpower.

ALPHABET SOUP

Can you tell the difference between the red and blue letters in each of the three groups of capital letters?

Two letters are missing from each group and they are outside the chalkboard as shown. Can you place these letters back into the groups in which they belong?

Answer on page 162

MYSTERY MESSAGE

Can you decipher the hidden message?

Answer on page 162

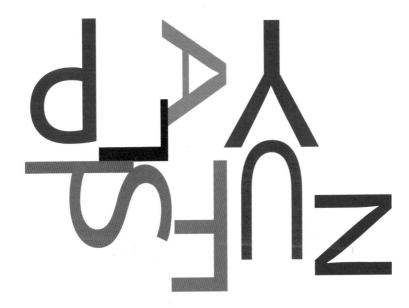

LEVEL 1

WORD MIX

Rearrange these letters to form a single word: **EAR IMPLANT**
Answer on page 162

CROSS WORDS

Can you rearrange the following sets of letters and place them in the grid below? One letter has already been placed for you. Can you find a theme to this simple crossword?
Answer on page 163

PUTSE
UMLG
NGREA
MUTRNTA

**L
E
V
E
L**

1

CROSS COUNTRIES

The six anagrams below represent three countries and their
capital cities. Can you unscramble them all and fit them into the grid?
Three letters have been placed for you.

Answer on page 163

LGAORPTU
GLOANA
LOSO
SLIONB
ANDALU
WORNYA

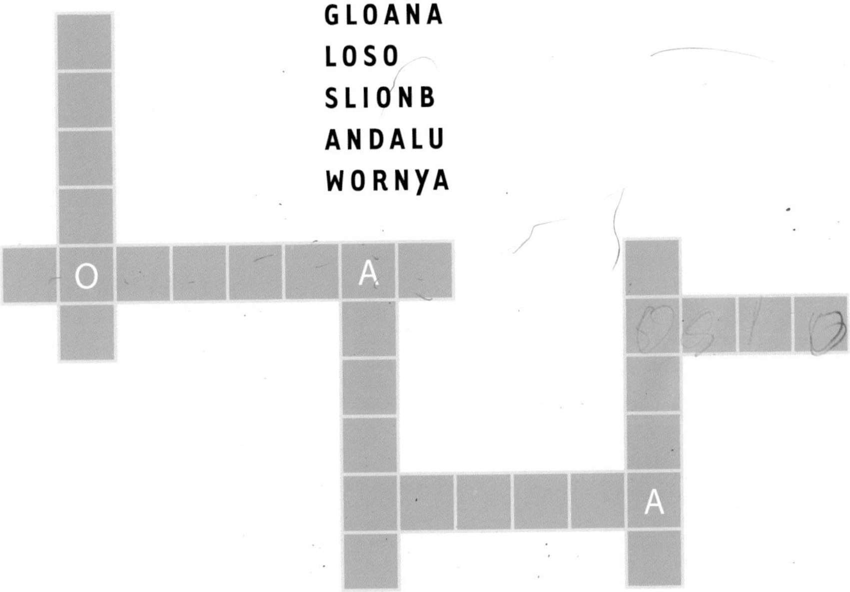

CIRCLE LOTTO

Just by looking, can you decipher this piece of advice?
Answer on page 163

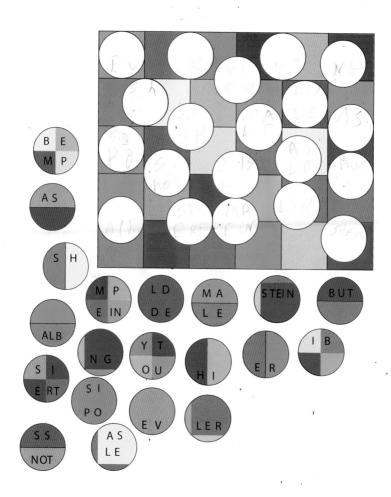

Can you decipher this *Grook*, as the short poems of Danish inventor, poet, and scientist Piet Hein are called?

Answer on page 164

LEVEL 2

SPLIT SAYING 1

These 13 trominoes can be rearranged to produce a saying by Sophocles. Can you find it?

Answer on page 164

R	I	T	R
H	U	O	R
C	U	E	I

A	E	A	L
H	O	H	N
E	W	H	R

				F
				T
				T

W	T	I	H
S	C	A	N
A	D	F	D

LETTER MAZE 1

Move from any square on the top row of the grid to any square on the bottom row by spelling out the names of countries. The last letter of each country must form the first letter of the following one in every case.

You can move up, down, and sideways in any direction, but not diagonally.

Answer on page 164

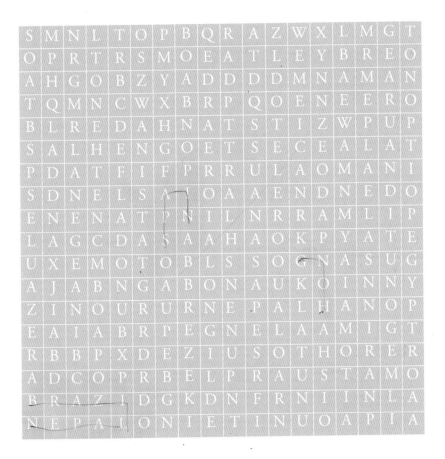

S M N L T O P B Q R A Z W X L M G T
O P R T R S M O E A T L E Y B R E O
A H G O B Z Y A D D D D M N A M A N
T Q M N C W X B R P Q O E N E E R O
B L R E D A H N A T S T I Z W P U P
S A L H E N G O E T S E C E A L A T
P D A T F I F P R R U L A O M A N I
S D N E L S A I O A A E N D N E D O
E N E N A T P N I L N R R A M L I P
L A G C D A S A A H A O K P Y A T E
U X E M O T O B L S S O G N A S U G
A J A B N G A B O N A U K O I N N Y
Z I N O U R U R N E P A L H A N O P
E A I A B R P E G N E L A A M I G T
R B B P X D E Z I U S O T H O R E R
A D C O P R B E L P R A U S T A M O
B R A Z I L D G K D N F R N I I N L A
N E P A L O N I E T I N U O A P I A

LEVEL 2

LETTER MAZE 2

Starting at the red circle, move around the lines of the grid to spell out a question without crossing your own path. If your question is correct, the remaining circles that you have not visited will spell out, in order, the answer to the question you have made. You may visit each circle once only.

Answer on page 165

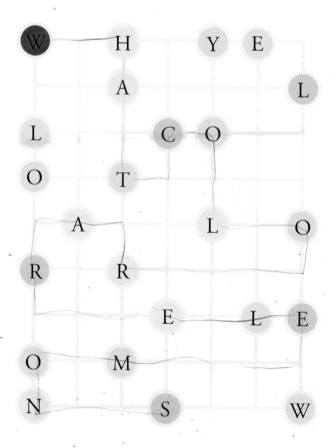

STACKED BLOCKS 1

The blocks each have a six-letter word written on them, but unfortunately you can see only three sides of each block. When you have solved the clues, the first column will reveal a 10-letter word.

Answer on page 165

CLUES

1. Outlaw
2. Clever
3. Brief downpour
4. Martial art
5. Flee
6. Boredom
7. Copper alloy
8. Bowman
9. Sheen
10. Toils

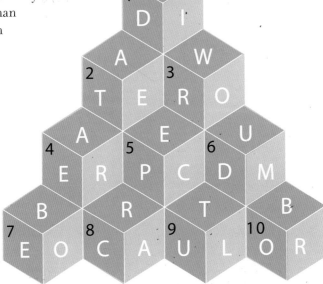

SPLIT SAYING 2

These pieces can be rearranged to produce a quotation. Can you find it?

Answer on page 165

WORD PATH 1

Can you find your way along the path by answering the clues below. Each word overlaps with the next (the last letter of each word also is the start of the next word).

Answer on page 166

1. Sunrise
2. Tidy
3. Semester
4. Repair
5. Medic
6. Correct
7. Three
8. Child with no parents
9. Like a wide-eyed innocent
10. Too much
11. Twenty
12. Wicked
13. Perfectly flat
14. One washing machine's worth

L
E
V
E
L

3

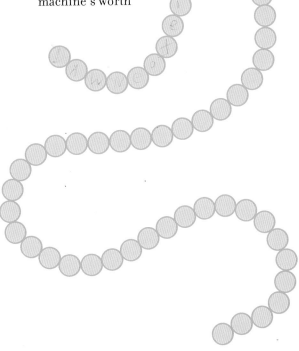

Five related letters have been encoded as different letters in the five points of the star. Using logic, can you reveal the original letters? The number in the middle of the star may help you.

Answer on page 166

NO EYE DEAR

There was a man who didn't have eyes. He went to the woods to view the skies. He saw a tree with apples on it. He didn't take apples off it, yet he didn't leave apples on it.

How could that be?

Answer on page 166

CUBIC CRYPTOGRAM

A message has been left on the map of Gridlock City for the spy. The hidden message can be read along the edges of a diamond with eight letters on each side. However, the instructions did not indicate where the center of the diamond is, just that it lies somewhere in the middle column of letters.

Answer on page 167

STATUS SYMBOLS 1

Can you work out which term matches which symbol on the cards marked 1–25?

Answers on page 167

And so on
Approaches (in value)
Approximately equal to
Circumference
Corresponds to
Diameter
Equal to
Equal to or greater than
Equal to or less than
Identically equal to
Infinity
Intersecting circles
Less than
Not equal to
Plus or minus
Radius
Rhombus
Scalene triangle
Sector
Segment
Similar to (proportional)
Square root
Sum of terms
Tangent
Therefore

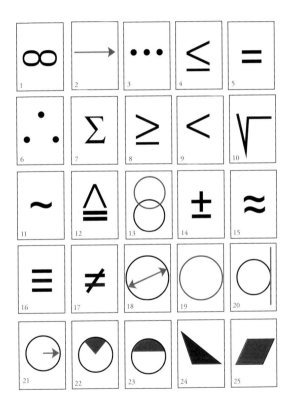

STATUS SYMBOLS 2

Can you work out which term matches which symbol on the cards marked 26-50?

Answers on page 168

Acute angle
Circle
Cone
Congruent to
Cube
Cuboid
Cylinder
Equilateral triangle
Isosceles triangle
Kite
Obtuse angle
Octahedron
Parallelepiped
Parallelogram
Pyramid
Regular heptagon
Regular hexagon
Regular nonagon
Regular octagon
Regular pentagon
Right angle
Right triangle
Sphere
Tetrahedron
Trapezoid

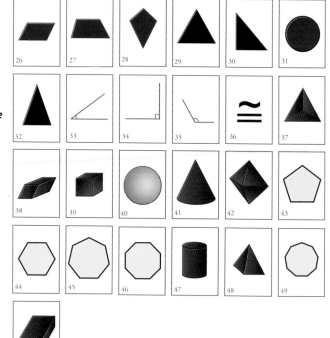

ANAGRAM GRID

In the first row the letters of the solution appear in a random order. The goal of the puzzle is to use the same letters to form different words in each row according to the number of blank cells available. An example using eight letters is shown.

You are not allowed to repeat words. Points are scored for each word you can find, plus an extra eight points for filling every square. What will you score on the 10-letter anagram grid?

Answer on page 168

An 8-letter sample anagram grid.

A sample solution scoring 21 points.

THE 10-LETTER ANAGRAM GRID.

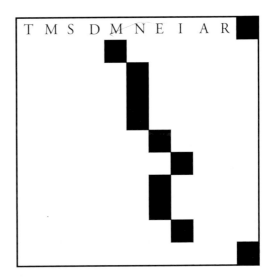

CODE STAR 2

Moving clockwise around the star, can you reveal the hidden five-letter name? What logic has been used to create the code?

Answer on page 169

STACKED BLOCKS 2

The dice blocks each have a six-letter word written on them, but unfortunately you can see only three sides. When you have solved the clues, the first column will reveal a 10-letter phrase.

Answer on page 169

CLUES

1. Hollow space
2. Install in office
3. Annul
4. Nook
5. Commotion
6. One of the Gorgons
7. Winner
8. Swallow up
9. Star cluster
10. Candle fat

LEVEL
5

WORD PATH 2

Can you find your way along the path by answering the clues below? Each word overlaps with the next with the last letter of each word also being the first letter of the next word.

Answer on page 169

1. A spider weaves one
2. Letter after alpha
3. Computer company named after a fruit
4. Finish
5. Catastrophe
6. Opposite of left
7. Threesome
8. One who always looks on the bright side
9. Couple
10. Possess
11. At no time
12. Tear apart
13. Starchy vegetable
14. Unusual
15. Tom-tom, for instance
16. Cut, as grass

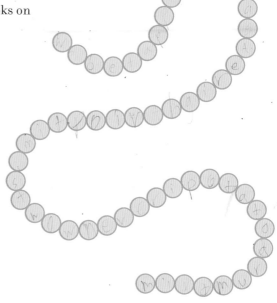

RIDDLE

Can you solve this riddle?

My first is in blue but never in glue,
My second's in old but never in new.
My third is in look but never in see,
My fourth is in ask but never in plea.
My whole has leaves and yet has no flower;
I will help you to pass an idle hour.
What am I?

Answer on page 170

NAME THAT GIRL

Four friends — Dolly, Diana, Irene, and Lynne – all discovered that their names had something unusual in common. It's not that they are all girl's names, which would be too literal. Nor is it that each of them contains two of the same letter, which would be too easy. What do you think it is?

Answer on page 170

L
E
V
E
L

5

SHARED ELEMENT

The following four items all have something in common. Can you tell what it is?

Answer on page 170

FACETIOUS

GATHERING CLOUDS

TRADE DISCOUNT

BATTLE IT OUT

LEVEL

5

ANSWERS

SHAPE UP

1. True

2. False

3. True only if the rectangle is a square

4. False (it quadruples)

5. True only if it is a square

6. True

7. False

8. True (it's a special case of a parallelogram—with all sides equal)

9. True if and only if no two are parallel, and no three lines pass through a single point, as shown below:

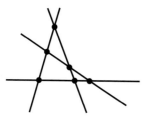

LOST IN SPACE

There are many ways the space station can be traversed according to the rules; one is shown.

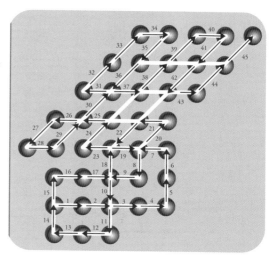

ALL ROADS LEAD FROM HOME

It helps to tilt the grid 45 degrees as shown for reasons to be explained. The point now at the top is "home."

Let's first consider why there may be more than one shortest route between two points in Gridlock City.

There is only one way to stay at home, so we put 1 in that position. There is exactly one way to go to each of the points in the next layer down, so mark 1s in those, too. Now consider the third layer.

The only way to get to its left corner is by the end of the layer above. But the middle position can be reached in two ways: either by the position above and to the left, or above and to the right. Then there is only one way to reach the right-hand end. So place the numbers 1, 2, 1 on the diagram. And so on.

By now you should have worked out the principle. The numbered triangle is the famous Pascal's triangle. In Pascal's triangle each number is the sum of the two numbers above it. This triangle has many applications in probability.

The two tan limiting routes are 20 units in length. There are many more routes, all inside the yellow square as shown. The final figure shows there are 184,756 possible routes.

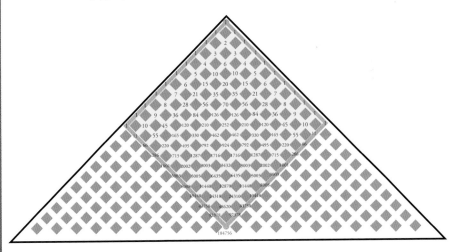

A WINDOW OF OPPORTUNITY

The new window is shown here.

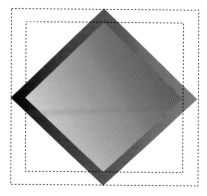

ELUSIVE ELLIPSE?

The man can pick up the glass of water, tilt it, and see the surface of the water forming a perfect ellipse.

INEBRIATED INSECT

Here, the "exploded view" shows the cylindrical glass flattened out into a rectangle. The shortest path involves the ladybug crawling upward to meet the edge halfway, then taking a similar path back down inside the glass. To calculate the length of the path: Circumference of glass = $\pi \times$ diameter, so the rectangle's width = 3.14 inches $\times$ 4 = 12.6 inches (approximately). The ladybug on the outside of the glass will travel half of this distance (6.3 inches) horizontally, and a total of 5.5 inches vertically. Via the Pythagorean theorem, we can therefore deduce the total distance traveled = square root of (6.3 squared + 5.5 squared) = 8.4 inches (rounded to one decimal place).

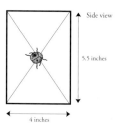

Side view

5.5 inches

4 inches

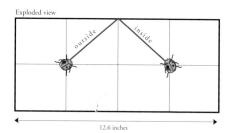

Exploded view

outside   inside

12.6 inches

PERFECT GOLOMB RULER: 4 MARKERS

A 6-unit length ruler with 4 markers is "perfect."

The 4 markers on a ruler of length 6 enable you to measure all consecutive distances from 1 to 6 between 2 markers in one way only.

Distance	Measure
1	0 to 1
2	4 to 6
3	1 to 4
4	0 to 4
5	1 to 6
6	0 to 6

SPHERE OF INFLUENCE

Volume of sphere = $4/3\pi r^3$

$= 4/3\pi(D/2)^3$ where D = diameter of sphere

$= 1/6\pi D^3$

$\pi/6 = 3.14/6 = $ approximately 0.52

Hence, water occupies 52% of the cube's volume, as shown.

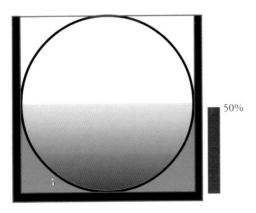

50%

GOT YOU PEGGED

As shown, six pegs will be left free.

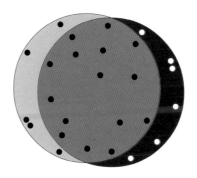

FLAG THE FLY

One of the many possible solutions is shown here.

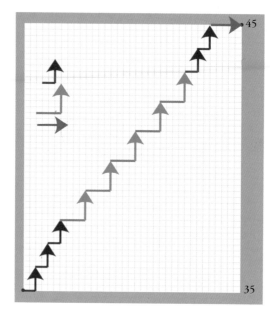

TRANSFORMABLE CYLINDER

While the lower disc rotates, the stretched rubber bands create an endless number of transformations—from the initial cylinder to families of hyperboloids and finally to a double cone. It is quite surprising to find that surfaces as distinctly curved as this can be formed purely from sets of straight lines.

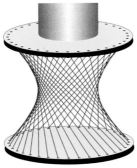

SCHLEGEL'S SHORTCUT

One possible solution to the problem is shown here on the Schlegel diagram.

TREASURE HUNT

You will need just one trial dig to pinpoint the treasure, since the treasure is hidden at one of the two intersection points of the two diamonds as circled here in red.

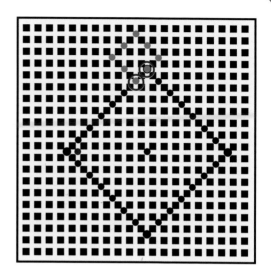

Deer, Oh Deer!

Dogged Determination

THE SHORT AND LONG OF IT

The longest path is shown below (lengths used are indicated within the yellow box). It measures 320 units in total. Very often simple analog gadgets can solve complex mathematical problems. Jos Wennmacker of the Netherlands devised a simple gadget that can solve our problem and even more complex problems of this kind in no time.

Wennmacker creates an analog model of the graph by knotting together pieces of string in exact scale (or connecting the pieces of string to small rings or eyelets). This is demonstrated below. The result is obtained by two simple operations. Pick up the string structure at any node (point) and let it hang freely. Pick up again at the lowest node and hang it again, and you have the longest path. It's as simple as that!

The selected node for the first step is shown with a red circle around it. The longest route is shown by the squares on the map (below).

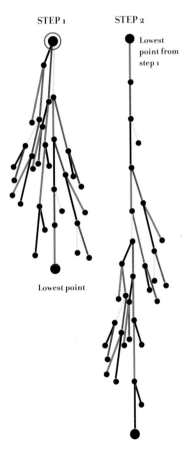

STEP 1

STEP 2

Lowest point from step 1

Lowest point

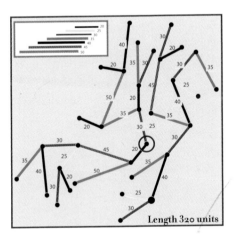

Length 320 units

PERFECT GOLOMB RULER TOO?

No, it's not a perfect ruler. In fact, no perfect Golomb rulers exist that are longer than 6 units. For longer rulers, either some distances occur more than once or some distances cannot be measured at all.

In our 11-length ruler with 5 markers, the length 6 cannot be measured, although all the rest can be, as shown below. It is the shortest optimum Golomb ruler for 5 markers.

Another 11-length ruler with one distance missing is shown below right. Here, the 10-unit length cannot be measured.

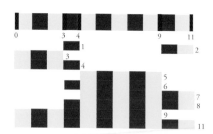

GANYMEDE CIRCLE 1

For clarity, distances are always measured clockwise around the circle.

Distance	Measure clockwise
1	A to B
2	B to D
3	A to D
4	D to A
5	D to B
6	B to A
7	Entire circle

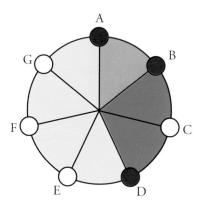

GANYMEDE CIRCLE 2

9 = 1 + 2 + 6
10 = 6 + 4
11 = 6 + 4 + 1
12 = 2 + 6 + 4
13 = Entire circle

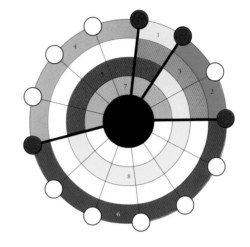

GANYMEDE CIRCLE 3

6 = 5 + 1
9 = 5 + 1 + 3
11 = 7 + 4
12 = 10 + 2
13 = 3 + 10
14 = 1 + 3 + 10
15 = 3 + 10 + 2
16 = 1 + 3 + 10 + 2
17 = 10 + 2 + 5
18 = 10 + 2 + 5 + 1
19 = 5 + 1 + 3 + 10
20 = 3 + 10 + 2 + 5
21 = Entire circle

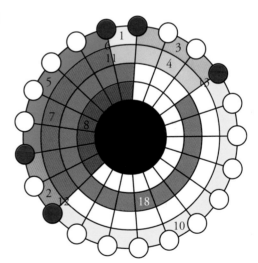

I SPY

The illegal alien spaceship entered from the top left planet and intended to leave from the lowest planet on the right, where it was intercepted by the waiting defense forces.

In the given graph, there are only two points with an odd number of routes connected to them. It can only be traced without crossing a route more than once if one of these points is the beginning and the other is the end. We know that the upper point is the entry and so the lower point is the only possible end of the route, or the potential exit point.

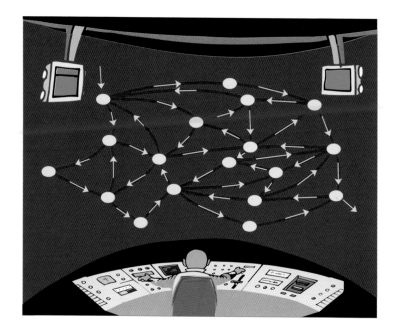

MONTY HALL PROBLEM

Martin Gardner has presented several versions of the "game show" paradox, which still pops up in different versions and disguises, but the *Parade* magazine columnist, Marilyn vos Savant, is most famously associated with it. Her 1990 column on the subject provided the right answer but provoked thousands of letters of disbelief and accusation.

Why? Because the answer seems so wrong and counterintuitive.

The correct method is always to switch. Suppose we choose door 1. The chart below shows how we win only one out of three times if we don't switch but can increase our chances to two out of three if we do switch.

NO SWITCHING
WINS 1 IN 3

SWITCHING
WINS 2 IN 3

THE MONK AND THE MOUNTAIN

This is an interesting problem whose visual representation leads to a fairly obvious solution.

No matter the speed of ascent and descent of the monk during his journeys, or how long he rested, or even if he traveled backward at times, his two paths must intersect at a point somewhere along the route. This is shown in the diagram below, in which the two paths are superimposed.

Here's another way to think about the problem:

Suppose that two monks are making the two journeys, one walking up and the other walking down at the same time. One starts from the bottom and the other starts from the top at the same time, seven in the morning. Both arrive at the end of their journey at seven in the evening. At some point they must meet regardless of their speed and how often each of them stops. This is the time and place we are asking for.

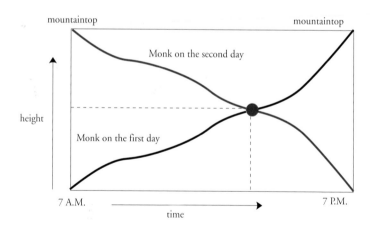

BANK RAID

This is how a Flatlander can open the vault and remove anything within it. On the other hand, a three-dimensional person could easily remove the gold without breaking or opening the sealed vault. By analogy, a four-dimensional person could achieve this feat in our world and empty all the gold stored in banks anywhere.

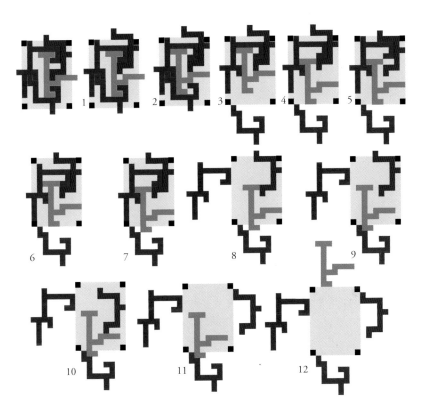

PICTURE STRIP

Rotate every strip by 180 degrees. The shaded squares will now be in the positions marked here in black. They form a simple picture of someone playing soccer.

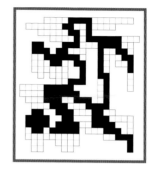

STAINED GLASS WINDOW

The missing panes are the group of five showing the blue sky in the background. Groups of five panes are always red, so these should be red, too (single panes are always black, groups of two always yellow, and so on).

RIGHT TO THE EDGE

Three colors are sufficient, as one of the possible solutions illustrated below shows.

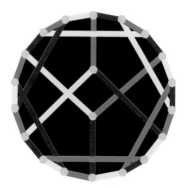

FIRE DRILL

If the middle rung is labeled "zero," then the fireman went up three rungs to number 3, down five rungs to number −2, then up seven rungs to number 5. Finally he went up six more rungs to the top.

So the top must have been 11 rungs above the middle. Add to this the 11 rungs below the middle, and the middle rung itself, and the answer is 23 rungs.

STARRY SKY

It has been proven that a convex pentagon can always be drawn in any configuration of nine randomly placed points. Eight points can be placed (as shown) without creating a convex pentagon. Any additional point will unavoidably create a convex pentagon.

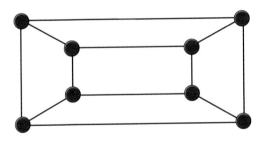

ALIEN-NATION

The first must have said "I'm an alien," for, if he is an alien, he can't tell a lie and, if he is a human being, he can't tell the truth. Therefore (2) is telling the truth and is an alien.

This results in two possible outcomes:

Alien–Alien–Human or Human–Alien–Alien

Conclusion: There are more aliens than human beings.

FAR TRAVELED

You will always be able to make round-trips.

For example, one New York round-trip may be:

New York—Phoenix—Houston—Anchorage—Orlando—Portland—San Francisco—New York.

ZOO-LOGICAL

Area 1 = 3 square units
Area 2 = 1.5 square units
Area 3 = 3 square units
Area 4 = 15.5 square units
Area 5 = 2.5 square units
Area 6 = 2.5 square units
Area 7 = 2 square units
Area 8 = 5 square units
Total area = 35 square units

CHOP CHOP

No. The division of cake 1 and cake 3 was equal, but the red pieces in cake 2 were bigger. If the number of chords (cuts) is even and equal to 4 or more, the areas (pieces) are always equal. Otherwise, there is a slim chance that the total areas of the red and yellow pieces will be equal (one chord must go through the center of the circle), but this is unlikely.

This puzzle was inspired by the "Pizza Problem" discovered by L.J. Upton in 1968; proven by Larry Carter and Stan Wagon in 1994.

(L.J.Upton, Problem 660, *Mathematical Magazine*, 1976; Stan Wagon, Problem 83, *The Mathematical Intelligencer*, 1983)

BE FLIPPANT

The probability of getting two tails and two heads in the order TTHH is the product of the individual probabilities:

$1/_2 \times 1/_2 \times 1/_2 \times 1/_2 = 1/_{16}$.

MOLE

The rule was: The mole goes forward one block then turns right, then forward two blocks then turns right, forward three blocks and turns right, and so on, until the mole counts up to nine blocks. The mole then starts over again. However, when he starts the fourth series of moves, he chooses to turn left twice, then right. That's the point where he breaks the rule (marked with a blue cross).

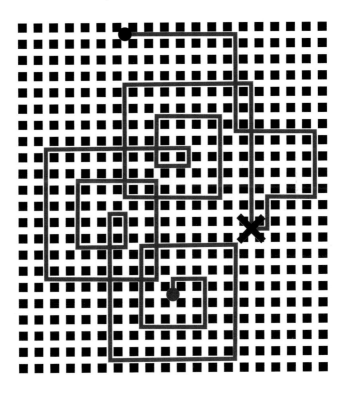

GLOBE-TROTTING

One possible solution.

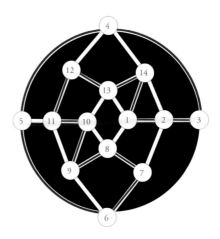

EULERIAN PATHS

We can conclude at the outset that the graph does not have an Eulerian circuit since it has two odd vertices (B and D).

However, we can start an Eulerian path at point B and finish at D, or vice versa. In creating the path we have to be careful not to make a move that would result in disconnecting the uncovered paths.

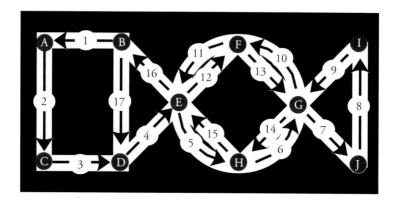

ONE FOR THE BIRDS

Three red birds (R) and two blue birds (B), as demonstrated below.

$R - 1 = B$

$3 (B - 1) = R$

Hence, $3B - 3 = B + 1$

$2B = 4$

$B = 2$

$R = 2 + 1 = 3$

RECONNAISSANCE

You can't do it!

After passing an odd number of intersections, you will be inside the boundary. To return to the starting point, you must have passed an even number of intersections. Thus the number can't be 11 or any other odd number.

HAPPY END PROBLEM

It takes five points, with no three of them in a straight line, to guarantee a convex quadrilateral.

This was elegantly proven by the Erdös-Szekeres theorem. If you surround the given points by a rubber band (like lassoing the points), there can only be three possibilities:

1. The band forms a convex quadrilateral (with the fifth point inside);
2. The band forms a pentagon—connecting two vertices of which will always result in a convex quarilateral;
3. The band will form a triangle, with two points inside. Draw a line through the two interior points—on one side will be one vertex, on the other will be two. Take the latter two vertices and the two interior points—these will make a convex quadrilateral.

PIPELINE PUZZLE

One possible solution.

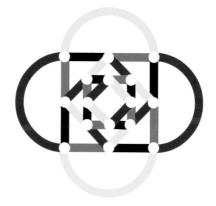

LOCAL LIQUOR

The way to find the average "best" location is to average the x-coordinates first, and then the y-coordinates:

Average of x = (1 + 1 + 1+ 3+ 4+ 6+ 7+ 7+ 8+ 10+ 11+ 12)/12 = 5.9
Average of y = (1 + 1 + 2 + 3+ 4 + 4 + 5 + 7 + 7 + 9 + 9 + 12)/12 = 5.3

Therefore the best place for the bar is (5.9, 5.3).
The nearest coordinate to this is at (6,5), which is point B.

T-HAT'S MAGIC!

In move 1, the worst possible scenario is to transfer four eggs of one color plus one of another color.

In move 2, the worst scenario would be to transfer all the red and green eggs, which would be nine eggs. To satisfy the requirement to have at least three eggs of each color in hat 1, you would need to account for the worst scenario and transfer 12 eggs, so if the magician did indeed move all nine red and green eggs, he would need to move three remaining eggs, which are yellow. So 12 eggs is the answer the audience must give to ensure the magician gets the result he wants.

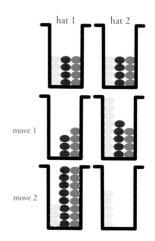

CATERING FOR THE CHILDREN

PUZZLE 1

The maximum number of pieces into which the three cakes can be cut by three, four, and five cuts (a total of 12 straight line cuts) is seven, 11, and 16 pieces respectively, a total of 34 pieces. So the answer is yes.

This solution is the minimal "best" solution, but there can be other solutions if more than two cuts (lines) are allowed to meet at a point: for example, cutting the cakes by two, four, and six cuts into four (max), eight, and 22 (max) pieces respectively.

This problem is a simple example from a branch of mathematics called combinatorial geometry, in which there is a fascinating interplay between shapes and numbers.

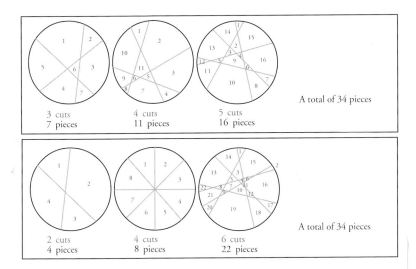

3 cuts
7 pieces

4 cuts
11 pieces

5 cuts
16 pieces

A total of 34 pieces

2 cuts
4 pieces

4 cuts
8 pieces

6 cuts
22 pieces

A total of 34 pieces

PUZZLE 2

With the requirement of cutting the cakes into identical pieces we have to cut each cake radially from the center into 12 pieces, making 36 pieces altogether (in which case there will be pieces of cake for you and me as well).

ID PARADE

Since Mac was in the middle of the lineup, an odd number of inmates took part. Since Jim was 20th, there must have been at least 21 inmates. Mac's position must have been an odd number lower than 13, so he was 11th and there were 21 inmates in line.

DELIVER THE GOODS

The schematic diagram below shows the minimum distance between every combination of locations in Gridlock City. For example, the shortest traveling distance between the red 3 and the red 5 is six blocks, so we label that line with a yellow 6.

The problem now becomes: Visit every red dot in a loop, collecting the smallest total of yellow numbers possible. Via a little trial and error, you'll find the shortest solution is 26 blocks, as shown by the arrows on the diagram.

By analogy, the best route on the original diagram (on page 50) is to visit the locations in this order (or its reverse): 1, 5, 6, 2, 3, 4, and back to 1.

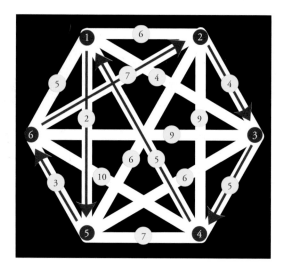

A SHAKER'S DOZEN

In general, "n" people each shake hands with "$n-1$" people (as one doesn't shake hands with oneself). Since two people share a handshake, this result must be halved to get the number of handshakes (H):

$H = n \times (n-1)/2 = (n^2-n)/2$

There were 66 handshakes, since $(12^2-12)/2 = 66$.

GOLDEN HANDSHAKE

The 17 members of the board were supposed to shake hands with 16 people, which would amount to $(17^2-17)/2 = 136$ handshakes.

But four people did not shake hands, so there were $(4^2-4)/2 = 6$ handshakes fewer, for a total of 130 handshakes.

(See "A Shaker's Dozen," above, for a full explanation.)

LET'S SHAKE ON IT

A 10-point graph can help (to demonstrate the 10 people involved).

Assume A had the maximum number of eight handshakes. J was left without a handshake, so must be the wife of A because we are told that spouses did not shake hands.

B had seven handshakes, and I must be the wife of B (with one handshake).

C had six handshakes, and H must be the wife of C (with two handshakes).

D had five handshakes, and G must be the wife of D (with three).

E had four handshakes, and F must be the wife of E having also had four handshakes.

It follows that I must be E, and F (my wife) had four handshakes as well.

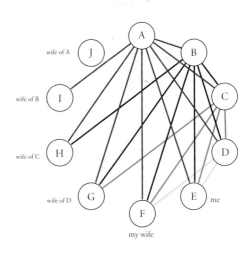

One solution is shown. For the other solution: In move 2, hiker 2 crosses back instead of hiker 1.

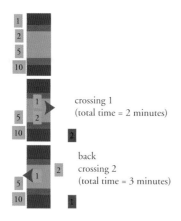

crossing 1
(total time = 2 minutes)

back
crossing 2
(total time = 3 minutes)

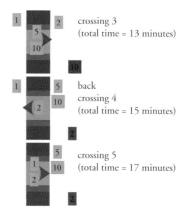

crossing 3
(total time = 13 minutes)

back
crossing 4
(total time = 15 minutes)

crossing 5
(total time = 17 minutes)

GET THE MESSAGE?

1 + 2 = 3

2 + 3 = 5

5 − 2 = 3

MAGIC ARROWS

One possible solution.

2	2	0	0	0	2
1	↘	←	→	↗	1
0	↑	↘	↗	↓	0
0	↑	↘	↘	↓	0
1	↘	←	→	↘	1
2	0	0	0	2	2

SWEEEET
Cake = $1.75; Sundae = $0.75

A SUITE DEAL?
She was wrong.

$1,200 is 125% of $960 (she made a $240 profit).
$1,200 is 80% of $1,500 (her loss was $300).
The combined sale had a loss of $60.

TIM'S TURTLE
A circle, or as near to a circle as you can get,
will always maximize the space available.

ST. IVES' RIDDLE
Only one.
   All the others were coming from St. Ives.

WHO IS A MILLIONAIRE?
1. The person who is 1,000,000 hours old is 114 years old.
2. The person who is 1,000,000 minutes old is about two years old.
3. The person who is 1,000,000 seconds old is a baby just over 11½ days old.
4. The woman must be the odd one out, as she is clearly none of these.

TOT UP A TON

There are many solutions. We give a few here. Can you find any others?

$$123 - 45 - 67 + 89 = 100$$
$$1 + 2 + 34 - 5 + 67 - 8 + 9 = 100$$
$$123 - 4 - 5 - 6 - 7 + 8 - 9 = 100$$

SCHOOL BUS 1

Three separate children could board the bus in six different ways. But with our restriction that two of the children board the bus one after another, the number of different ways they can board the bus is: $2 \times 2 = 4$. That's because the groups can board the bus two ways: the pair first or the single child first, and the pair can board two ways: older child first or younger child first.

SCHOOL BUS 2

Four separate children could board the bus in 24 different ways. But with our restriction that two of the children board the bus one after another, the number of different ways they can board the bus is: $6 \times 2 = 12$.

Five children under the same restriction can board the bus in $24 \times 2 = 48$ ways.

THE FIRST CONTACT

$1 + 2 = 3$ (true)
$2 + 3 = 5$ (true)
$5 - 2 = 3$ (true)
$3 + 2 = 4$ (false)

A convincing proof that the message was understood.

SNAIL'S PACE

The snail ends up 4 units higher after each day and night. After 20 full days, it will be 20 × 4 units = 80 units up the window, after which there are only 10 units left to travel. So on day 21 it will easily reach the top and that's it—there's no need to consider the slide back. So 21 days is the answer.

GOLDEN JUBILEE

Taking into account the Pythagorean relationship, the amount of gold in the two smaller plaques is the same as in the big one. So there is no difference.

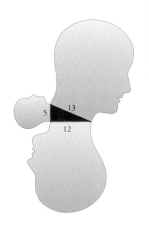

It is a lesser-known fact that the Pythagorean theorem holds for any set of geometrically similar figures drawn on the three sides of a right-angled triangle.

The validity of this so-called generalized form of the Pythagorean theorem relates not only to areas but also to the volumes of the figures if their thicknesses are identical.

SKYDIVING 1

Four separate skydivers could jump from the airplane in 24 different ways. Following the restriction that three of them always jump one after the other, the number of different ways they can jump is 2 × 6 = 12. (The three skydivers can jump in six different ways, and can jump before or after the single skydiver.)

SKYDIVING 2

Five separate skydivers could jump from the airplane in 120 different ways. Following the restriction that three of them always jump one after the other, the number of different ways they can jump is $6 \times 6 = 36$.

Following the same restrictions six skydivers can jump in $24 \times 6 = 120$ ways.

PUZZLE WITH A TWIST

Imagine that you unwrap the cylindrical building and flatten it as shown.

According to the Pythagorean theorem:
$c^2 = a^2 + b^2 = 30^2 + 40^2 = 900 + 1,600 = 2,500$ units.

Hence, $c = \sqrt{2,500} = 50$ units.

Therefore, the staircase length is $4 \times 50 = 200$ units.

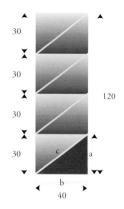

AN UP AND DOWN CAREER

It is possible to visit all floors of the building (up journeys are shown in light blue, down journeys in dark blue).

The minimum number of journeys to visit all floors is, of course, 19 and the floors will be visited in the following sequence:

1–9–17–6–14–3–11–19–8–16–5–13–2–10–18–7–15–4–12–20.

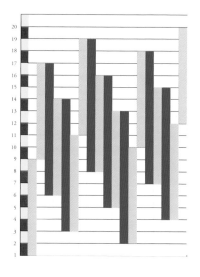

PIPE BAND

The band consists of four curved sections and four straight lines. The four curved sections are each ¼ of a circle. Since the circumference of a circle = $\pi \times$ diameter, these total $\pi \times 1 = \pi$. Each straight line = $2d = 2$. Hence the total = $8 + \pi$ units, or about 11.14 units.

THE SHOELACE PROBLEM

The zigzag lacing uses the least lace, leaving you with the longest bow when you tie your shoe, so it's the most efficient. The straight lacing comes next, followed by the quick lacing.

If we don't have to alternate through the eyelets on the left and right sides of the shoe, even shorter lacings such as the bow tie are possible.

COMMUTER COMPUTATION

You might think that you can add up the speeds and average them, like so: $(28 + 56)/2 = 42$. Unfortunately, it isn't that simple.

No matter what the distance between home and office, the average speed is 37.28 mph.

To work it out, suppose that the journey to work took one hour; the return journey would naturally take two hours. Therefore I traveled 111.8 miles in three hours, which gives the answer above.

GRASSHOPPING

The next two complete jumps are $n = 9$ and $n = 13$, as shown. The latter can be expressed as: $1 + 2 - 3 + 4 + 5 - 6 + 7 - 8 + 9 - 10 + 11 - 12 + 13 = 13$.

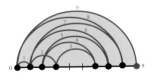
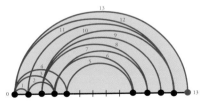

THE SAFE SAFE

There are 26 letters in the alphabet and four letters will be chosen for the combination lock, so you multiply $26 \times 25 \times 24 \times 23 = 358,800$ in order to obtain the number of permutations.

Since it takes five seconds to try each permutation, it would take nearly 500 hours to be sure of finding the right one!

SKELETON CUBES

We can choose a color for each side in turn, that is, $12 \times 11 \times 10 \times \ldots \times 3 \times 2 \times 1 = 479,001,600$. However, the cube can lie on six sides and each side can face upward in four orientations, so the true number of different cubes is $(479,001,600) \div (6 \times 4) = 19,958,400$.

HISTORY MYSTERY

This is perhaps the world's oldest puzzle. The solution is the geometric progression of five terms, of which the first term is 7 and the multiplier is also 7:

houses	7
cats	49
mice	343
ears	2,401
flour	16,807 (the answer)

PLANT PLOT

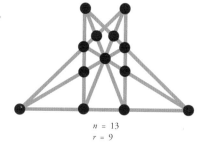

$n = 13$
$r = 9$

PLAYGROUND

The highest point is shown in black. It is
on the only plank that is slanted and not
parallel to the ground as are all the rest.

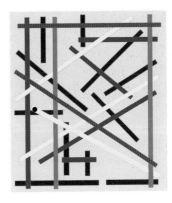

THE CIRCLE INSIDE

All the black regions have the same area. It is simple to see that three of
the diagrams are the same except that the parts of the circle have been
rearranged. The third diagram (bottom left) contains one quarter of a
circle that has twice the radius of the circle in the other diagrams. Since
area = πr^2, the area is also identical.

MYSTERY SHAPE

The missing shape is number 8

   The rest of the number sequence from 1 to 9 appears rotated and in
mirror image.

HERE'S THE PLAN 1

A–4

HERE'S THE PLAN 2

B–4

LINEUP

1 − 17	13 − 10
2 − 14	14 − 11
3 − 3	15 − 2
4 − 24	16 − 20
5 − 15	17 − 25
6 − 18	18 − 16
7 − 7	19 − 19
8 − 5	20 − 21
9 − 4	21 − 9
10 − 8	22 − 23
11 − 13	23 − 22
12 − 1	24 − 12
	25 − 6

FELINE A BIT PECKISH

All nine birds can be swallowed by the cat, as shown.

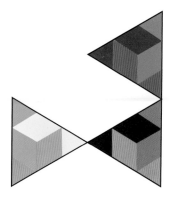

TO THE MAX

All the triangles have the same area, since they have equal bases and the same perpendicular height.

HERE'S THE PLAN 3

C−1

HERE'S THE PLAN 4

D−4

CHEESE, PLEASE

Imagine all three cubes of cheese lie on a horizontal table. In the first cube, you will always obtain a square if you take a slice that's parallel to the table.

If you tilt up the cube by 45 degrees, so that only one edge touches the table, more shapes are possible. Depending on the height of the cut you take, the resulting slices will range from squat to tall rectangles.

Now tilt the cube again so that only one point of the cube touches the table and the diametrically opposite corner is vertically above it. This time, the first slices you take will mostly be triangles. However, nearer the middle you will obtain some hexagons and, at one point halfway up, the slice will be a perfectly regular hexagon. (To see why, note that the lines are the same length because they all run from the middle of one side of the cube to the middle of another side. Hence, it's a regular hexagon.)

The two pentagons shown in the question are impossible to obtain.

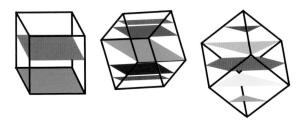

HIDDEN POLGYONS

9 squares   8 squares

2 octagons   1 octagonal star

1. A
2. D
3. D

HERE'S THE PLAN 5
E–4

HERE'S THE PLAN 6
F–4

THE HINGED SQUARE
The square will become an equilateral triangle.

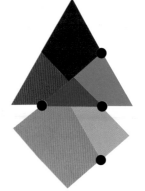

PAPER VIEW 2
1. C
2. B
3. C

TWENTY-FIVE SENSE
Here we show a solution with 34 connecting lines. Six potential lines were left unconnected. Can you do better? If not, do you know why not?

LADYBUG IN HIDING

The leaves can be considered as nodes (points) of a graph. If a leaf has an even number of boundary crossings (overlaps with other leaves), the ladybug can enter and leave it, whereas a leaf with an odd number of boundary crossings can be entered and left by the ladybug but, when it reenters, it cannot leave again.

This means that the only leaf with an odd number of crossings is the leaf under which the ladybug ends its journey and hides. Drawing a line through all the leaves that have only two crossings, and marking the multiply crossed leaves, you can easily complete a continuous line through all the leaves, never retracing the line.

A maze like this can be traversed if only zero or two of the leaves have an odd number of adjacent leaves. If it's zero, you can start anywhere because it's a closed loop. If it's two, those two leaves are the start and finish points. That's what we have in this case—the start point has one adjacent leaf, and the finish point has three adjacent leaves. All the others have even numbers of adjacent leaves.

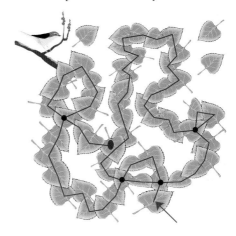

SWEET SIXTEEN

Among the 14 different possible solutions (not counting rotations or reflections as different), there are two symmetrical patterns, and four solutions with the smallest number of intersections (two).

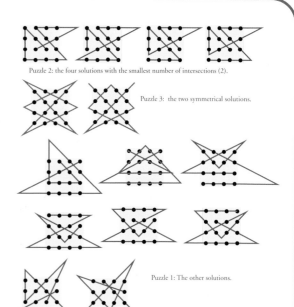

Puzzle 2: the four solutions with the smallest number of intersections (2).

Puzzle 3: the two symmetrical solutions.

Puzzle 1: The other solutions.

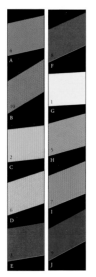

BLANKET COVERAGE

It's actually a regular octagon that has been repeated many times.

STOPGAPS

A	4
B	10
C	2
D	6
E	3
F	8
G	1
H	5
I	7
J	9

FOUR-WAY MAZE

The bottom arrow leads to the shortest path to the center.

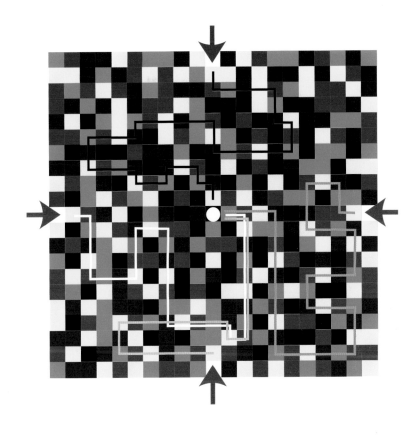

ALPHABET SOUP

Group 1: The red letters are capital letters of the alphabet with vertical symmetry. The blue letters are those with horizontal symmetry.

Group 2: The blue letters are capital letters of the alphabet with both horizontal and vertical symmetry. The red letters are asymmetrical capital letters with no closed areas.

Group 3: The red letters are asymmetrical and contain closed areas. The blue letters have no bilateral symmetry, but have a two-fold rotational symmetry.

Some letters may have no bilateral symmetry (no line that will dissect them into two mirror-halves), but still possess rotational symmetry.

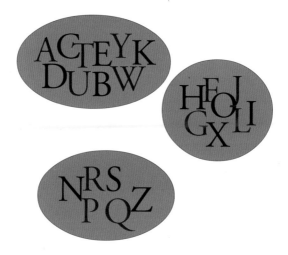

Mystery Message

The letters are rotated in place, spelling the sentence "Play is fun."

Word Mix

The answer is Parliament.

CROSS WORDS

All the words are associated with the emotion of anger (or "cross," if you forgive the pun).

CROSS COUNTRIES

CIRCLE LOTTO

If you fit the circles into the rectangle so the colors match, you get this piece of advice:

"Everything should be made as simple as possible, but not simpler."

—Albert Einstein

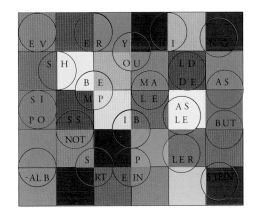

POETRY CIRCLE

"A bit of virtue will never hurt you."

The sentence is formed by taking the letters in order of increasing size.

SPLIT SAYING

"Rather fail with honor than succeed with fraud."—Sophocles

R	A	T	H	E	R	F	A	I	L	W	I	T
H	H	O	N	O	R	T	H	A	N	S	U	C
C	E	E	D	W	I	T	H	F	R	A	U	D

LETTER MAZE

Germany, Yemen, New Zealand, Denmark, Korea, Australia, Albania, Afghanistan, Netherlands, Senegal, Luxembourg, Gabon, Nepal, Lesotho, Oman, Niger, Romania.

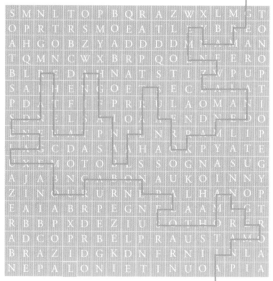

Letter Maze 2

Question: What color are lemons?
Answer: Yellow

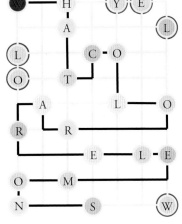

STACKED BLOCKS 1

1. Bandit
2. Astute
3. Shower
4. Karate
5. Escape
6. Tedium
7. Bronze
8. Archer
9. Lustre
10. Labors

First Column: Basketball

Split Saying 2

"Victory always starts in the head."—Douchan Gersi

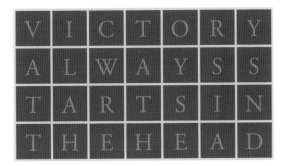

WORD PATH 1

Dawn
Neat
Term
Mend
Doctor
Right
Trio
Orphan
Naïve
Excess
Score
Evil
Level
Load

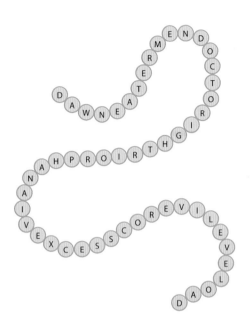

CODE STAR 1

Beginning at the top point the letters are alternately −5 and +5 away from the five vowels: A, E, I, O, and U.

NO EYE DEAR

The answer lies in taking the use of plurals literally. The man had only one eye (so he didn't have "eyes"). The tree had only two apples on it. He took only one, and left only one on the tree (so he didn't leave "apples").

CUBIC CRYPTOGRAM

The spy's message is revealed here: "BETRAYED—LEAVE—GRIDLOCK—NOW!"

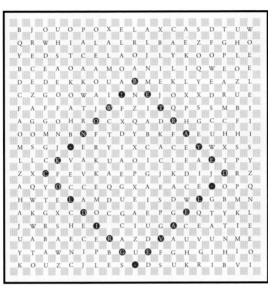

STATUS SYMBOLS 1

1. Infinity
2. Approaches (in value)
3. And so on
4. Equal to or less than
5. Equal to
6. Therefore
7. Sum of terms
8. Equal to or greater than
9. Less than
10. Square root
11. Similar to (proportional)
12. Corresponds to
13. Intersecting circles
14. Plus or minus
15. Approximately equal to
16. Identically equal to
17. Not equal to
18. Diameter
19. Circumference
20. Tangent
21. Radius
22. Sector
23. Segment
24. Scalene triangle
25. Rhombus

STATUS SYMBOLS 2

26. Parallelogram
27. Trapezoid
28. Kite
29. Equilateral triangle
30. Right triangle
31. Circle
32. Isosceles triangle
33. Acute angle
34. Right angle
35. Obtuse angle
36. Congruent to
37. Tetrahedron
38. Parallelepiped
39. Cube
40. Sphere
41. Cone
42. Octahedron
43. Regular pentagon
44. Regular hexagon
45. Regular heptagon
46. Regular octagon
47. Cylinder
48. Pyramid
49. Regular nonagon
50. Cuboid

ANAGRAM GRID

The grid shows a score of 26 points. Other answers are possible.

T	M	S	D	M	N	E	I	A	R	
T	R	I	M		A	M	E	N	D	S
T	R	I	M	S		N	A	M	E	D
D	R	E	A	M		M	I	N	T	S
S	M	A	R	T		D	E	N	I	M
M	I	N	T	E	D		R	A	M	S
M	I	N	D	S	E	T		A	R	M
T	A	N	D	E	M		R	I	M	S
M	A	D	M	E	N		S	T	I	R
D	I	M	M	E	R	S		A	N	T
M	A	S	T	E	R	M	I	N	D	

Code Star 2

If each letter is given a number value (assuming A=1) and added together, the resultant number is again equal to its corresponding letter. Hence HH = 8 + 8 = 16 = P. Continuing in this fashion the name **PETER** is revealed.

STACKED BLOCKS 2

1. Cavity
2. Invest
3. Revoke
4. Corner
5. Uproar
6. Medusa
7. Victor
8. Engulf
9. Nebula
10. Tallow

First Column: Circumvent

WORD PATH 2

1. Web
2. Beta
3. Apple
4. End
5. Disaster
6. Right
7. Trio
8. Optimist
9. Two
10. Own
11. Never
12. Rip
13. Potato
14. Odd
15. Drum
16. Mow

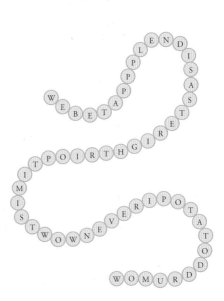

RIDDLE
The answer is book.

NAME THAT GIRL
They are all anagrams of boys names: Lloyd, Aidan, Ernie and Lenny.

SHARED ELEMENT
Each of the phrases contains the five vowels in order of their appearance in the alphabet without repetition.

facetious

gathering clouds

trade discount

battle it out

GENIUS GYMNASIUM TRAINING PROGRAM
The Moscovich Method for Mental Muscle

WEEK 1

Puzzle Type: Puzzle Name	Level	Record your time
Day 1		
Creative Thinking: Shape Up	Level 1	
Logic Puzzles: Stained Glass Window	Level 1	
Number Puzzles: Get the Message?	Level 1	
Visual Reasoning: Playground	Level 1	
Word Games: Alphabet Soup	Level 1	
Day 2		
Creative Thinking: Lost in Space	Level 1	
Logic Puzzles: Right to the Edge	Level 1	
Number Puzzles: Magic Arrows	Level 1	
Visual Reasoning: The Circle Inside	Level 1	
Word Games: Mystery Message	Level 1	
Day 3		
Creative Thinking: All Roads Lead from Home	Level 1	
Logic Puzzles: Fire Drill	Level 1	
Number Puzzles: Sweeeet	Level 1	
Visual Reasoning: Mystery Shape	Level 1	
Word Games: Word Mix	Level 1	
Day 4		
Creative Thinking: Window of Opportunity	Level 1	
Logic Puzzles: Starry Sky	Level 1	
Number Puzzles: A Suite Deal?	Level 1	
Visual Reasoning: Here's the Plan 1	Level 1	
Word Games: Cross Words	Level 1	
Day 5		
Creative Thinking: Elusive Ellipse?	Level 1	
Logic Puzzles: Alien-Nation	Level 1	
Number Puzzles: Tim's Turtle	Level 1	
Visual Reasoning: Here's the Plan 2	Level 1	
Word Games: Cross Countries	Level 1	

WEEK 2

Puzzle Type: Puzzle Name	Level	Record your time

Day 1

Creative Thinking: Inebriated Insect	Level 2	
Logic Puzzles: Far Traveled	Level 2	
Number Puzzles: St Ives' Riddle	Level 2	
Visual Reasoning: Lineup	Level 2	
Word Games: Circle Lotto	Level 2	

Day 2

Creative Thinking: Perfect Golomb Ruler	Level 2	
Logic Puzzles: Zoo-Logical	Level 2	
Number Puzzles: Who Is a Millionaire?	Level 2	
Visual Reasoning: Feline a Bit Peckish	Level 2	
Word Games: Poetry Circle	Level 2	

Day 3

Creative Thinking: Sphere of Influence	Level 2	
Logic Puzzles: Chop Chop	Level 2	
Number Puzzles: Tot Up a Ton	Level 2	
Visual Reasoning: To the Max	Level 2	
Word Games: Split Saying 1	Level 2	

Day 4

Creative Thinking: Got You Pegged	Level 2	
Logic Puzzles: Be Flippant	Level 2	
Number Puzzles: School Bus 1	Level 2	
Visual Reasoning: Here's the Plan 3	Level 2	
Word Games: Letter Maze 1	Level 2	

Day 5

Creative Thinking: Flag the Fly	Level 2	
Logic Puzzles: Mole	Level 2	
Number Puzzles: School Bus 2	Level 2	
Visual Reasoning: Here's the Plan 4	Level 2	
Word Games: Letter Maze 2	Level 2	

WEEK 3

Puzzle Type: Puzzle Name	Level	Record your time
Day 1		
Creative Thinking: Transformable Cylinder	Level 3	
Logic Puzzles: Globe-Trotting	Level 3	
Number Puzzles: The First Contact	Level 3	
Visual Reasoning: Cheese, Please	Level 3	
Word Games: Stacked Blocks 1	Level 3	
Day 2		
Creative Thinking: Schlegel's Shortcut	Level 3	
Logic Puzzles: Eulerian Paths	Level 3	
Number Puzzles: Snail's Pace	Level 3	
Visual Reasoning: Hidden Polygons	Level 3	
Word Games: Split Saying 2	Level 3	
Day 3		
Creative Thinking: Treasure Hunt	Level 3	
Logic Puzzles: One for the Birds	Level 3	
Number Puzzles: Golden Jubilee	Level 3	
Visual Reasoning: Paper View 1	Level 3	
Word Games: Word Path 1	Level 3	
Day 4		
Creative Thinking: Deer, Oh Deer!	Level 3	
Logic Puzzles: Reconnaissance	Level 3	
Number Puzzles: Skydiving 1	Level 3	
Visual Reasoning: Here's the Plan 5	Level 3	
Word Games: Code Star 1	Level 3	
Day 5		
Creative Thinking: Dogged Determination	Level 3	
Logic Puzzles: Happy End Problem	Level 3	
Number Puzzles: Skydiving 2	Level 3	
Visual Reasoning: Here's the Plan 6	Level 3	
Word Games: No Eye Dear	Level 3	

WEEK 4

Puzzle Type: Puzzle Name	Level	Record your time
Day 1		
Creative Thinking: The Short and Long of It	Level 4	
Logic Puzzles: Pipeline Puzzle	Level 4	
Number Puzzles: Puzzle with a Twist	Level 4	
Visual Reasoning: The Hinged Square	Level 4	
Word Games: Cubic Cryptogram	Level 4	
Day 2		
Creative Thinking: Perfect Golomb Ruler Too?	Level 4	
Logic Puzzles: Local Liquor	Level 4	
Number Puzzles: An Up and Down Career	Level 4	
Visual Reasoning: Paper View 2	Level 4	
Word Games: Status Symbols 1	Level 4	
Day 3		
Creative Thinking: Ganymede Circle 1	Level 4	
Logic Puzzles: T-Hat's Magic!	Level 4	
Number Puzzles: Pipe Band	Level 4	
Visual Reasoning: Twenty-Five Sense	Level 4	
Word Games: Status Symbols 2	Level 4	
Day 4		
Creative Thinking: Ganymede Circle 2	Level 4	
Logic Puzzles: Catering for the Children	Level 4	
Number Puzzles: The Shoelace Problem	Level 4	
Visual Reasoning: Here's the Plan 7	Level 4	
Word Games: Anagram Grid	Level 4	
Day 5		
Creative Thinking: Ganymede Circle 3	Level 4	
Logic Puzzles: ID Parade	Level 4	
Number Puzzles: Commuter Computation	Level 4	
Visual Reasoning: Here's the Plan 8	Level 4	
Word Games: Code Star 2	Level 4	